AF240885

United Arab Emirates
Conquering the World

Max Milo, Paris, 2023

www.maxmilo.com

ISBN : 978-2-315-01133-9

Sébastien Boussois

UNITED ARAB EMIRATES
CONQUERING THE WORLD

Max Milo

ESSAIS - DOCUMENTS

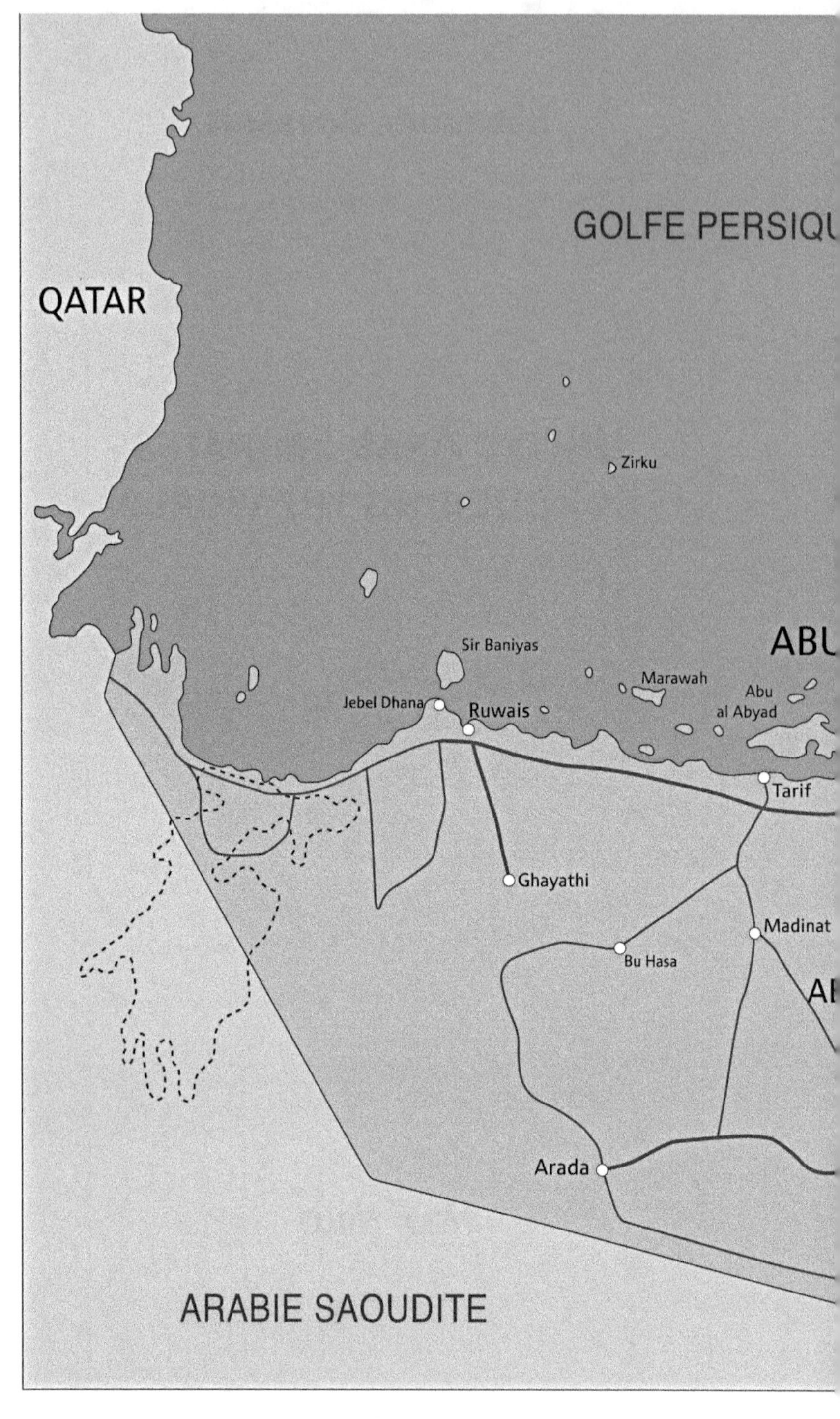

QATAR
GOLFE PERSIQU
Zirku
Sir Baniyas
Marawah
Abu
al Abyad
ABU
Jebel Dhana
Ruwais
Tarif
Ghayathi
Madinat
Bu Hasa
AI
Arada
ARABIE SAOUDITE

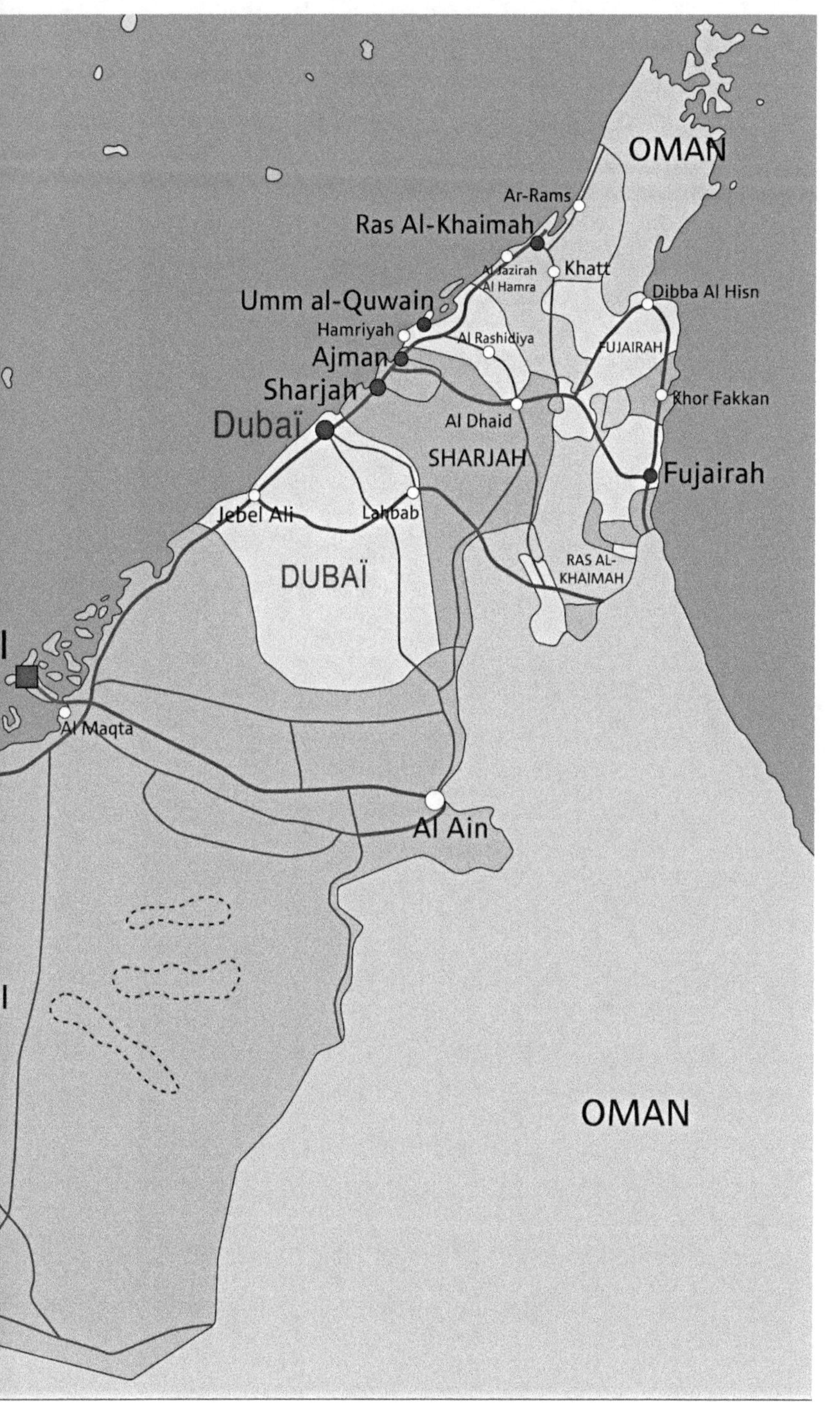

OMAN
Ar-Rams
Ras Al-Khaimah
Khatt
Al Jazirah
Al Hamra
Dibba Al Hisn
Umm al-Quwain
Hamriyah
Al Rashidiya
FUJAIRAH
Ajman
Khor Fakkan
Sharjah
Dubaï
Al Dhaid
Fujairah
SHARJAH
Jebel Ali
Lahbab
DUBAÏ
RAS AL-
KHAIMAH
Al Maqta
Al Ain
OMAN

Introduction

In 2019, Abu Dhabi and Dubai lined up a record that may seem superficial: the "Flowers of Tolerance" is now the largest natural flower carpet in the world. And one more whimsical record for the United Arab Emirates (UAE), one, after those, among others,

- of the largest empty picture frame in the world,
- of the largest hand-woven carpet,
- of the largest number of people dressed as mummies in three minutes,
- of the biggest Christmas ball,
- of the largest image of a human coffee maker,
- of the largest parasol on the planet,
- of the largest cup of hot tea in the world,
- of the largest number of LED lamps installed on a public road,
- of the largest gold ring,
- of the largest human image of a flag,

- of the largest book,

- of the largest sword,

- of the largest wheelchair race,

- the fastest police force in the world, and

- of the highest proportion of men in a country compared to women (218 men for 100 women)...

These titles may seem trivial, and they are - not all of them, if you add to them the Khalifa Tower, known as the Burj Khalifa, the "tallest human structure ever built" at 828 meters. Yet all of them have a strong geopolitical meaning. They have been gleaned precisely because they were nonsensical. By their incongruity and accumulation, they maintain the perception of a facetious, light, open Emirate, forming a liberal island in the middle of the archipelago of conservative Gulf monarchies. Seen in this light, Abu Dhabi deserves to be, according to the slogan of the World Expo 2020, "the center of the world for 182 days"[1]!

The combination of sparkle and unconcealed ambition is the hallmark of the UAE. It is also reflected in the way the Emirates have invested Brussels, the capital of the European Union and the headquarters of the North Atlantic Treaty Organization. Indeed, after years of obvious disinterest, the Gulf countries have returned without skimping on resources. The Emirates' embassy is located in the Delune house, at 86, avenue Franklin Roosevelt in Ixelles, one of the most beautiful avenues in the capital, which is home to many foreign embas-

---

1. https://www.expo2020dubai.com/fr

sies and listed buildings. The place is magnificent: it is one of the most famous examples of Art Nouveau architecture in Brussels. On the large green boulevard, it is impossible to miss this mixture of Western and Byzantine influences, located not far from the Saudi Arabian and Qatari embassies. However, two steps away, the former Emirati embassy, less flamboyant but twice as big, houses the military office of the embassy.

But in December 2020, the small, hushed and flourishing world of the Emirati enclave was rocked by a scandal. *La Dernière Heure* revealed a massive fraud, dating back *at least* forty years and accompanied by acts of moral harassment - one witness described a diplomat as "a tyrant" who "demolished" him[2]. According to the elements pointed out by the investigation, the embassy forgot - oops!- to declare its workers between its arrival in 1976 and 1994. More than that, once its crime was revealed, it continued to work illegally, making only partial declarations for certain employees and continuing to blithely violate Belgian labour legislation.

Like the association between nonsense and geopolitical ambition, the great discrepancy between the architectural beauty of the embassy and the sordid reality of what goes on there is a good summary of what the UAE has become, *id is* a magnificent façade concealing a noria of obscure practices. More than obscure: black, even, sometimes. Such a dichotomy, which attempts to hide unacceptable practices through

---

2. https://www.dhnet.be/actu/belgique/harcelement-moral-au-coeur-de-l-ambassade-des-emirats-arabes-unis-de-bruxelles-il-a-agi-comme-un-tyran-nous-a-demolis-5fda59e97b50a652f7a1fd9b

bluster and the spectacular, should be beyond the pale. Unfortunately, it does not prevent the United Arab Emirates from continuing to spread their web in the capital of the European Union, as much with the powerful of this world as with the ordinary people.

This is evidenced by the popularity of influencers - especially French - for Dubai. Many stars of the genre have taken up residence there. Among them, ladies from reality TV like Nabilla, a shampoo specialist if ever there was one, Caroline Receveur, who went from *Secret Story* to selling detox tea, or Jessica Thivenin, for whom cosmetic surgery has no secret since she had it done to reshape her breasts, teeth, lips and chin (*work in progress*). In their wake, the European Francophonie has followed the hexagonal movement and has also gone into exile: for example, the Belgian DJ Daddy K and the Swiss Jean-Pierre Fanguin went to see if the sand was more golden. In his polished videos where camels and buggies criss-cross a superb desert, the Swiss YouTubeur even promotes the Emirates, praising the good life, luxury, wealth and easy money.

Let's forget for a moment the iconography likely to make dream the housewife of less than fifty years old who vibrates - at least sporadically - in many of us, and let's ask ourselves why these entrepreneurs opted for such a delocalization. More than the change of scenery or the fiscal interest, all of them are delighted by the discretion and the incomparable luxury that Dubai offers them: they enjoy the possibility of not being recognized in their daily life, while they are scrutinized by millions of *followers*. As a bonus and at no extra cost, the voluntary exiles benefit from the modern, exotic and sunny image of the Emirati city. As they, in turn, maintain this myth, it's a *win-win* for their hosts. Thanks to the influencers, the UAE maintains its image *via* social networks where these instrumentalized individuals prolong the mirage of an open, free and fulfilling country.

In situ, the reality is less glittering. For ten years, all basic rights have been annihilated one by one in the Emirates. Now, its dignitaries are trying to extend the zone of influence of their seemingly clean dictatorship. Two pretexts are used to justify this policy: on the regional level, political stability; on the global level, the fight against terrorism. In the shadow of the glittering skyscrapers and the Western imagination fed with images of free people, easy access to alcohol and bikini parades on the beaches of Dubai, the current political and ideological center of the Emirates is located in Abu Dhabi, where a family has taken power: the Al Nahyan.

The influence of this royal family accelerated sharply in 2008, after Dubai's economic collapse due to the financial crisis and the collapse of a highly speculative real estate market. Abandoned by Abu Dhabi, Dubai was forced to relinquish much of its constitutional power to the rising dynasty. Within that family, one man has emerged as the dominant figure: Crown Prince Mohamed bin Zayed, whose obsession with oversight and control of the regime has gradually become the reason for statehood in the emirates. The fear of the Arab Spring has accentuated this trend.

However, MBZ's desire for stability has not stopped at the UAE's borders. In the Arab world as a whole, Abu Dhabi has supported repressive regimes in Egypt and Libya in the name of the convenient fight against terrorism. Yet, it all fits together! In 2017, the blockade of Qatar, which will last until the "stability and solidarity" agreement signed on January 5, 2021, strengthens the ties between Saudi Arabia and the Emirates; and the support to the kingdom of Yemen, is nothing but an attempt to mute both the backers of the 2011 uprisings and Al Jazeera, which had been the mouthpiece of the revolutionaries. MBZ has thus served as an ideological mentor to Saudi Crown Prince Mohamed bin Salmane, with whom he maintains a personal friendship. This strong bond lays the foundation for a bilateral alliance between Riyadh and Abu Dhabi, which is meant to serve as a bulwark against the other powers they support.

In Yemen, Riyadh and Abu Dhabi have found an object of desire that serves both ideology and power interests. While the UAE has officially arrived to help the kingdom fight the Houthi militia, an army of mercenaries and surrogates, led by MBZ, is waging a shadow war against the *Al-Islah* party (part of the Muslim Brotherhood) and its partners. At the same time, the uae has secured access to the most important ports along the southern shores of the Indian Ocean.

Elsewhere, it is the same story. On the other side of the Horn of Africa, the uae is able to pursue its regional great power ambition: in Somalia, Djibouti and Eritrea, it has massively expanded its aggressive hold on the ground. MBZ's experience in Egypt and Libya confirms that armed force can be successfully used to enforce neo-conservative ideologies and secure geopolitical interests through the use of disappearances, torture and targeted killings.

MBZ's crusade against the democratic gains of the "Arab Spring" threatens the stability of the region. The myth of the authoritarian solution lays the foundation for a short-term strategy that denies the socio-political reality of the Arab world since 2011. Abu Dhabi believes that repression can channel the individual's aspiration for social justice and political participation. On the contrary, the repression of this order provides fertile ground for extremism, particularly Islamist, insurgency and the outbreak of new revolutions. The island of freedom and modernity that the uae has seemed to be since 1971, when it gained independence, is now sinking into a radical security drift in a tense regional political context, between
- unilateral blockade against Qatar,
- bloody war in Yemen,
- assassination of the Saudi journalist Jamal Khashoggi,
- conflagration with Iran,
- attacks on Saudi facilities by Houthi drones,
- constitution of a sulphurous emirate-saudi-american-israeli axis,

- destabilization of the Arab revolutions and

- setting up a regional counter-revolution led by the UAE in order to favor the emergence and maintenance of military dictatorships.

How, with such a track record, can MBZ sometimes be considered the *leader of* the Arab world?

The geostrategic position of his country is not without reason. The UAE is located opposite the Strait of Hormuz and Iran. It is impossible to neglect it, complicated to shake it. Especially since the country has developed a vision for the development of its country, from the design of a regional and global *hub*, through the emergence of a futuristic city and an economic power like Dubai. Facing this city, and in a more political way, Abu Dhabi has developed and wants to develop its dual status as a military power and a regional arms hub. Since then, the UAE has been a privileged partner for the West, the United States and Europe. Thus for France, with which it maintains a relationship that is, to say the least, troubled.

In the ambitious, hard-line perspective that drives the prince, there is no quarter given. Qatar, which has refused to join the UAE since 1971, has been used as an example of what happens to the rebels. This is essential because the uae is constantly expanding its area of influence in all Muslim countries, including Egypt, Algeria, Sudan, Morocco, Tunisia and Iran. Now Abu Dhabi can realize its maritime dream as well by positioning itself at strategic points in the Gulf and the Indian Ocean. Its successes are boosting its ogre-like appetite and pushing it to advance its pawns, between *soft* and *hard power*, in India, China and Africa. There are almost no limits to MBZ's plans: in July 2014, the federation launched the Emirates Mars Mission. Now, on Feb. 9, 2021, this U.S.-backed project succeeded in placing the Al-Amal [hope in Arabic] probe into Martian orbit, making the UAE the fifth nation to settle around the red planet.

In appearance, a new and impressive step towards great power status. In reality, a new incentive in the project of transforming a confetti of British empire into the Great United Arab Emirates, which guides Mohamed ben Zayed, inclined to implement, for ten years, a policy of the powder keg that announces new dangers. This is what this book seeks to expose by showing how the rise of the Emirates has allowed him to develop a daring spirit of conquest whose prospects are both spectacular and potentially disturbing.

1. From pearl to oil

On the incense and silk road, located at a world geostrategic crossroads, the Arabian Peninsula has always been the object of all covetousness. Americans, French and English, the great Empires of the 19th century, were not mistaken. They launched great expeditions to conquer a profitable elsewhere. Alas for them, the local tribes, numerous in the region, made resistance! The Bani Yas, the Abu Al Falah and the Al Nahyan reigned over small territories which they did not intend to cede control to the invaders. It took many battles before the British, who arrived in the 1820s, imposed their rule in the so-called Trucial Coast states. In 1892, these territories were given the status of protectorates in the British Empire.

In this oil-rich region, the British competed with the Americans for local interests. However, it was not until 1960 that the richest oil deposits were discovered in Abu Dhabi. Sheikh Zayed Ben Sultan Al Nahyan, who founded the United Arab Emirates after independence in 1971, reigned there. In the 1960s, there was still a string of small emirates: Abu Dhabi, in the west, which was the largest, and Dubai stuck to it, to which were added those of Ajman, Charjah, Fujeirah, Raïs el Khaymah and Umm el Qaïwan. It is from the confederation of these seven former emirates that the well named United Arab Emirates was born.

However, two former Trucialist countries resisted and did not want to join the confederation: Bahrain and Qatar. While everyone was trying to agree on the terms of the future union, Qatar declared its independence on September 3, 1971. Its recognition by the international community was not long in coming, and the small Emirate promptly joined the United Nations and the Arab League. Its desire for emancipation remains a thorn in the side of the Emirates, and the source of a historical dispute that still agitates the region.

Within the UAE, each emirate has its own institutions and resource management, but foreign affairs, security and defence, education, emigration and health are the responsibility of the federal government. The capital of the emirates is Abu Dhabi. The president of the confederation is Sheikh Khalifa bin Zayed Al Nahyan; the vice-president and prime minister is Mohamed bin Rashi Al Maktoum, Emir of Dubai. The distribution of roles according to families is still the same. The emirate system consists of a supreme council, a council of ministers, a parliament, a federal national council and a judiciary. The supreme council elects the president and vice-president and has legislative and executive powers.

The confederated emirates are all equal, but some are less equal than others! The most important is Abu Dhabi, whose emir was elected president in 2004. Power is passed from father to son. This has allowed Mohamed bin Zayed, crown prince of the richest emirate in the confederation, to become the strongman of the entire confederation. It is thus the Al Nayan dynasty which is at the origin of the development of the United Arab Emirates since their independence. Zayed Ben Sultan Al Nahyan, founder of the country and nicknamed "the wise man of the Arabs", built both a fine fortune and a solid reputation by relying on two pillars: tradition and moderation.

Thus, it has begun an unprecedented process of modernization and openness, including a number of measures in favor of women's rights and education, as well as schooling and employment - enough to reassure Westerners, for whom the country is strategic. Indeed, nearly a quarter of the world's hydrocarbon supply passes through the Strait of Hormuz. While Qatar bathes in the middle of the Arabian Sea and has a single land border with Saudi Arabia (closed since 2017), the United Arab Emirates adjoins Saudi Arabia and also faces the Persian Gulf, the Strait of Hormuz and the Indian Ocean. This shows the interest in guaranteeing the stability of commercial waterways and having privileged relations with the emirate.

Since the Islamic revolution in 1979 and the first war between Iran and Iraq from 1980 to 1988, the Persian Gulf has been under tension and divided between Sunni allies (Saudis, Qataris, and Emiratis) and, on the other side, the Iranian

1. From pearl to oil

enemy. In order to preserve the billions of dollars that flow in every year to the whole world, Abu Dhabi is developing its energy and military *hard power in* the face of external threats. Supported by Westerners who depend on Hormuz for their energy autonomy, the Emirates are making sure they secure their pre-squared area in the face of the Iranian scarecrow. At the same time, a model of economic development is taking shape to mask the growing military imperative, thanks to oil, considered a gift from heaven.

Nihil novi sub sole: since the 16th century, the Emirates has been a land of trade that brings together people and goods, which structures its society. Indeed, as André Bourgey has explained,

> the emirates' long-standing commercial tradition, linked to close relations with the countries of the Indian ocean, allowed the emergence of a privileged social class, made up of shipowners and large merchants. Until the arrival of oil revenues, these merchant families held the economic power, while the ruling families were often economically dependent on the merchant class, and sometimes even had to borrow money from them. But the signing of oil concessions and the subsequent exploitation of black gold radically altered this situation by strengthening the power of the emirs and their families to the detriment of the rich merchant families.

It didn't all start with oil: for more than a century, the main wealth of the region remained pearl farming, renowned worldwide for its quality. Then this trade withered away until the advent of cultured pearls produced by Japan dealt a fatal blow. The "Trente Glorieuses" changed the situation. Under pressure from Western countries, in full industrial expansion, and therefore panicked at the idea of a disruption of oil and natural gas supplies, the intensification of the search for hydrocarbon deposits led to the discovery of a *jackpot*... with an essential geopolitical consequence.

> Oil has allowed the consolidation of the fragile political entities that are the Gulf petro-monarchies. The search for and exploitation of hydrocarbon deposits have led to the affirmation of the notion of borders, whether land or sea, in a region that had never before had a precise border.[3]

In 1960, the British discovered the first major oil field in what would become the United Arab Emirates 11 years later. By 2020, the country was estimated to have 6% of the world's oil reserves, compared to Qatar's 2%.

In the 1970s, at the time of its independence, the UAE took advantage of the oil shocks to dramatically increase its revenues and initiate the country's development. The region was nonetheless prone to conflict. For example, during the war

---

3. André Bourgey, "L'Histoire des Émirats Arabes du Golfe", *Hérodote* magazine, 2009/2, n°133.

1. From pearl to oil

between Iran and Iraq (1980-1988), the Emirates and Saudi Arabia supported Saddam Hussein against the mullahs' Iran. It was not until the 1990s that the UAE embarked on a broader development program, anticipating the post-oil era through a planned diversification of the economy.

After independence, the urgency was to ensure political, economic and social stability; twenty years later, it is necessary to think about development in depth.

2. From the vision to the miracle city

To anticipate the decrease of the hydrocarbon rent, it is necessary to plan the diversification of the economy, as Philippe Boulanger summarizes it.

The rise of the United Arab Emirates has accelerated since the 1990s. It is apparent in all areas, from a political point of view, through the search for stability of the absolute monarchy, to an economic and urban point of view, by attracting investments that participate in the construction of new poles anchored in the globalization of exchanges, to a socio-cultural point of view, by giving Emiratis a standard of living equivalent to, or even superior to, that of the most developed countries in the world.[4]

In 2006, two years before the Qatari, Sheikh Mohamed ben Zayed Al Nahyan launched a major development program, the Abu Dhabi Economic Vision 2030. The goal?

---

4. https://www.persee.fr/doc/bagf_0004-5322_2012_num_89_1_8249

The economic progress of the Emirate through the establishment of a common framework aligning all policies and plans and fully involving the private sector in their implementation.

1. Conduct a comprehensive assessment of the key drivers of economic growth.

2. Create a comprehensive long-term economic vision, with explicit goals, to guide the evolution of Abu Dhabi's economy through 2030. The year 2030 represents a significant milestone for the Emirate of Abu Dhabi. The baseline growth assumptions reveal that Abu Dhabi could achieve tangible levels of economic diversification by then.[5]

Faced with the risk of a shortage of oil and gas, the emirate's priority is to propose a sustainable economic development model. This includes seven stages:
- Establishment of an integrated, efficient, and open market in the country;
- implementation of tax rules adapted to the economy;
- installation of a monetary and financial system favorable to investment;
- support for the labor market and the establishment of a favorable immigration policy, adapted to future needs;

---

5. https://www.actvet.gov.ae/en/Media/Lists/ELibraryLD/economic-vision-2030-full-versionEn.pdf

- training of the workforce and strengthening the attrac-
tiveness of the country for skilled workers and brains;
- infrastructure development; and
- underpinning the financial markets.

In this sevenfold perspective, the articulation between the private and public sectors must allow
- to boost the private sector and competition,
- to establish a sustainable economy in all transparency,
- to increase international relations and exchanges with as many countries as possible,
- support quality education, including bringing the world's most prestigious university campuses to the UAE, as well as
- to accentuate the unceasing struggle for the security of the country and the maintenance of its traditional values, culture and heritage.

Among the most successful economic ventures that have become powerful *soft power* tools are the city of Dubai, the Dubai Port World Authority, the world's third largest port operator, and the airlines Etihad and Emirates. These three elements are consubstantially linked. However, nothing predestined the city to such a development... except its underground. Run since the end of the 19th century by the Maktoum family, originally from Bani Yas, Dubai first specialized in pearl farming. In the 1960s, Emir Maktoum aspired to offer its inhabitants a modern city thanks to the first gas fields discovered on site. Then the idea of creating a city-state, like Hong Kong or Singapore, from a small fishing village, flourished.

The success is there. The city has grown from a few hundred thousand inhabitants in the 1970s to nearly three million today. On its four thousand square kilometers, towers are growing, and even growing very high: the Burj Khalifa tower culminates at 838 meters, forming, as it has been reported, the highest human structure ever built. In the 2000s, for those who can afford it, it has become a popular tourist destination for its excess and surrealism, and the official showcase of the UAE. Green, blue, with the appearance of Central Park, it has unique leisure parks such as Palm Islands and The World, hotels more incredible than the others (such as the Burj el Arab), shopping malls offering the most prestigious brands in the world and a police force circulating in luxury cars.

Let's face it: Dubai is not just window dressing. Its international airport was inaugurated in 1979. Since then, it has become one of the world's largest *hubs* in terms of traffic. Emirates is one of the most prestigious airlines in the world. Rachid Ben Saeed Al-Maktoum realized that in order to promote his new city to the world, he had to bring the world to it. To do so, it was necessary to offer the world's tourists a prestigious airline that would transform Dubai into a global *hub* and that would offer them a prestigious stopover in the Emirates on their long-haul flights. In 1985, Emirates was born out of these imperatives, when Dubai was not yet a global city. Today, the airline is the largest in the Middle East and the largest in the Emirates, ahead of Etihad - based in Abu Dhabi, a serious competitor. In 2013, Emirates carried 43 million passengers to over 400 destinations worldwide.

In addition to air traffic, Dubai has become a key location for global maritime traffic of goods and hydrocarbons. Its port, Jebel Ali, is unique in the world. Built in the 1970s, it sees the work of more than 5,000 companies registered in 120 countries pass through its quays. eIt is the largest man-made port and the 9th largest in the world in terms of traffic: one million cubic meters of containers every year. Dubai Port World (DPW), a merger of the Dubai Port Authority and its international extension DPI Terminals, has become a reference in the field and now manages many ports around the world.

In 2016, DPW claimed a turnover of more than $4 billion, and was the third largest port operator thanks to the 50 or so maritime supply terminals under its control in Africa, Europe, the United Kingdom, Canada, China, Russia and Oceania. Only the port of New York (or almost) escaped in 2006. Officially, security reasons were invoked. Haouas Taguia, a researcher at the Al Jazeera Center for Studies, tends to think that the reason for this failure is probably due to another of Dubai's specialties: money laundering.

3. From embezzlement to the de Croÿ affair

Dubai is a tax haven for some, an emirate with less than transparent financial practices for others. We will mention three of them: the traceability of flows, real estate speculation and money laundering.

The first point is sadly illustrated by the laundering of funds paid by the international community to help countries in crisis that are struggling to recover. This is the case of the "dramatic mismanagement" that has befallen Afghanistan, as Gilles Dorronsoro called it in an interview he gave me in May 2021. Many corrupt elites have embezzled the colossal amounts of money paid by international aid to fight the Taliban and restore the rule of law. The destination of these huge amounts of money is Dubai and its maze of discreet accounts. As a result, while Kabul is being handed over to the Taliban and Daech, Dubai is gorging itself with funds that are supposed to help fight the Taliban.

In a study by Brian George, published by the Carnegie Endowment for International Peace, the author explains how, for two decades, billions of dollars have flowed from one country to another without the U.S. taking any notice. Or,

These outflows have played a role in slowing Afghanistan's economic and political development, facilitating the resurgence of the Taliban and exacerbating regional instability. They have also largely negated the effects of the enormous amounts of development assistance and stabilization funds spent by the international community in Afghanistan. These critical observations are evidenced by the multitude of illicit financing cases and credible reports that highlight the cross-pollination of crime between Afghanistan and Dubai. There is perhaps no case that better illustrates these links than the notorious Kabul Bank scandal.

In a few words, let's recall this sordid story. In August 2010, the bank's executives and a handful of politicians were accused of having embezzled nearly a billion dollars through fraudulent loan schemes. Obvious examples have become famous, such as the emblematic case of Ahmad Zia Massoud, Afghan vice president in 2009, who was arrested in Dubai with a whopping $52 million in cash on his person[6]. A decade later,

---

6. https://www.theguardian.com/world/2010/dec/02/wikileaks-elite-af-ghans-millions-cash

timid recovery efforts have let hundreds of millions of dollars evaporate both into thin air, thanks to corruption, and into the city, as some of these fortunes were used to acquire real estate assets, particularly in Dubai.

Yet the ignominy had been brewing for decades, Brian George reminds us in his report.

> In the late 1990s, the service that handled money transfers between Russia, Central Asia and Afghanistan, and the Russian authorities began to suspect that it was a money laundering scheme - a fact unknown to the Afghan authorities - when a new intermediary named Farnood obtained a banking license from Kabul Bank. Farnood fled Russia but, aware of the opportunities in Dubai, he set up his general trading company there around 1996. In 1998, he obtained a foreign exchange license from the UAE Central Bank. With the help of a handful of employees, Farnood quickly established himself as one of the region's leading financial channels between Afghanistan and Dubai.

In the years following the international community's adventure in Afghanistan in 2001, Farmood and others realized how much they could profit from the confused rush to modernize Afghanistan's infrastructure and economy. (...) [It is likely that Farmood] wanted to borrow (in other words, embezzle) money from hapless depositors and then invest it

3. From embezzlement to the de Croÿ affair

in real estate in Dubai, and to launder the ill-gotten gains of corrupt, high-level clients.[7]

The link between real estate speculation and toxic bank assets has had more local but no less dramatic consequences, even slowing down the city's previously irresistible development. Indeed, the mortgage crisis has had very concrete repercussions. For example, construction of the iconic Burj Dubai and Burj Khalifa towers came to a halt for a time because of a lack of money... which had to be raised in Abu Dhabi. The banks lost billions in bad investments initially located in the United States. How did it come to this?

Dubai's banking system is highly connected to the international system. For a long time, it was only interested in one asset: real estate. But this obsession can *crash at* any time. In 2008, in the *New York Times,* Robert F. Worth explained the mechanism.

> Banks are lending less, and business finances and construction projects are suffering. The price of crude oil has fallen [on october 8, a barrel of oil was close to 80 dollars in London]. The region's stock markets have been in decline since June [and have been in free fall in recent days: since 5 October, the Dubai stock market has lost a quarter of its value, mainly because of the fall in real estate values].

---

7. https://carnegieendowment.org/2020/07/07/kabul-to-dubai-pipeline-lessons-learned-from-kabul-bank-scandal-pub-82189

On September 22, after repeatedly saying that the Gulf region, thanks to its oil wealth, was safe from the foreign financial crisis, the Central Bank of the United Arab Emirates released $13.6 billion to support the credit market, echoing the rescue measures adopted in the United States. But some bankers are already saying it won't be enough.

Some of the most extravagant projects - huge shopping malls, islands and other indoor ski resorts - are likely to be abandoned if they have not already found financing. The credit crunch could also put a damper on demand as would-be buyers find it increasingly difficult to get a loan.

This slowdown will be even more pronounced if the situation in the West worsens. Real estate prices for sale and rent, which have remained stable until now, are expected to start falling soon. At the same time, investor confidence has been dented by a long string of business scandals, jeopardizing Dubai's dreams of becoming the financial capital of the region.[8]

In 2008, the city's credit volume was growing at 49% per year. Deposits were not keeping up. The real estate economy was doing well but was in danger of collapsing, and the increase in contracted business, buildings that had to grow

---

8. https://www.courrierinternational.com/article/2008/10/08/dubai-la-bulle-immobiliere-menace-d-exploser

3. From embezzlement to the de Croÿ affair

from the sand, all facilitated the development of unscrupulous speculators. Borrowing, selling before the construction was even completed, and sometimes double or triple dipping in a few months: the money invested, received without control, contributed to the accentuation of corruption, bribes, embezzlement and financial scandals.

Years of spending in several key sectors had a cost that Dubai could no longer bear at the time of the crisis. It was therefore necessary to reschedule the debt contracted by DP World and Nakheel, a real estate investment subsidiary, and then to ask Abu Dhabi for a loan of ten billion dollars. This financial and moral weakening of Dubai opens a boulevard for Mohamed ben Zayed. The Maktoum clan played with fire and got burned. To reassure international allies and investors, it was time to impose a less liberal, more traditional and more secure counter-model, both in its protection system and in its economic and banking system. However, a less risky banking system is not *ipso facto* a healthy banking system.

Witness - this is the third part of this chapter - the "Dubai papers" affair that shook the city in May 2018. A leak brings to light Hélin, a company domiciled in Dubai and headed by Prince Henri de Croÿ. The man manages the fortune of hundreds of companies and personalities. The documents reveal the existence of tens of thousands of accounts hidden for years and held, in their own right or *via* a system of intermediaries, by Russian footballers and oligarchs, in order to take advantage of a tax optimization useful to the lucky owners of tens of millions of euros. Henri de Croÿ, who has already been prosecuted for tax fraud, is said to have contributed to the evaporation of nearly 84 million dollars. The Belgian State has filed a civil suit, but the case illustrates the parallel financial circuits of Dubai, aiming at attracting and absorbing as fast as possible capital coming from all over the world through various tricks such as

- the creation of *off-shore* companies,
- the circulation of *cash* without restriction of amounts upon arrival in the UAE,
- issuing false invoices and
- the multiplication of shell companies from Europe.

Is the UAE and Dubai a tax haven? It would seem so, but to push further in terms of taxation, it was Dubai that institutionalized the system for its own development. The state was weak but rich, hence the need to encourage investment through various incentives such as

- Facilitated issuance of residence permits,
- the multiplication of free zones with a tax floor,
- the absence of taxes, especially on wealth, and
- the absence of social charges.

Many elements remind us of the two discriminating criteria, according to the OECD, to define a tax haven, such as zero taxation and low control of incoming capital. As Sofia Farhat explains,

> even if, in theory, the UAE is a signatory to OECD standards to fight tax evasion and money laundering

3. From embezzlement to the de Croÿ affair

such as Base Erosion and Profit Shifting (BEPS) and the Common Reporting System (CRS), in practice, many companies manage to escape a concrete control of their activities and take refuge in a tax environment that suits them...[9]

Since the de Croÿ affair, nothing has changed. The Emirates returned to the European Union's blacklist of tax havens, along with eight other countries; and since then, it has regularly gone back and forth between the grey and black lists.

---

9. https://www.opinion-internationale.com/2019/05/08/retour-des-Émirats united-arabes-on-the-black-list-of-tax-havens-which-are-reasons-and-which-perspectives_61069.html

4. From arming to *land grabbing*

Nothing dramatic for Dubai because, in its eyes, the countries of the European Union are not the priority of priorities. It likes to point to its biggest clients, biggest markets, biggest potential: India, Pakistan and China. But if the city is interested in the world, the world is also interested in it. In 2018, it is estimated that more than 163 nationalities invested a total of $162 billion in real estate in the city. That year, "the Dubai Land Department, revealed that 39,802 transactions were recorded during the period, including 25,473 sales worth more than AED 56.6 billion [Emirates dirham, worth just over 0,2 €], approximately 11,000 mortgage transactions worth more than AED 86 billion, and another 3,486 transactions worth AED 19.3 billion [an average *deal* at more than AED 5.5 million, or about €1.2 million]. " The breakdown of traders was as follows.

Indian investors represented the largest base by nationality with 4,676 investments worth AED 8.6 billion, close to UAE investors with 4,112 investments worth

AED 9.4 billion. Saudi investors ranked 3e with 1,882 investments worth AED 3 billion, followed by Pakistanis with 1,851 investments worth AED 2.3 billion. British residents ranked 5e with 1,761 investments worth AED 3.4 billion, with the top 10 completed by Chinese, Egyptians, Jordanians, Canadians and Russians.[10]

However, fearing that a crisis may be brewing, Dubai has relaxed its laws even further. The city now allows foreign investors to own the entire capital of a UAE-based company. Until 2018, the host country had to retain 51% ownership. According to some journalists, Dubai is doing quite well and has boosted foreign investment, which is mainly regional.

According to the International Monetary Fund's forecast, economic growth in the Emirates is expected to slow further in 2017, after falling from 3 percent in 2016 to 1.3 percent in 2017. In Dubai, real estate sales slowed by 5-10% in 2017. But Abu Dhabi can count on its international popularity: in 2017, according to the International Institute of Finance, the country received $11 billion in foreign direct investment, 22 percent more than in 2016.[11]

---

10. https://www.thefirstgroup.com/fr/news/investors-commit-441bn-to-dubai-s-property-market-in-2018/
11. https://www.capital.fr/economie-politique/investisseurs-etrang-ers-loperation-seduction-des-Émirats Arabes Unis-1288999

It takes a superior sense of balance to accommodate, on the one hand, the investors who demand opaque optimization, and, on the other hand, the allied countries that demand, with varying degrees of firmness, more transparency. Among these friends is France, a nation with nearly 30,000 workers based in Dubai, a permanent member of the United Nations Security Council and a major arms dealer. But Abu Dhabi is going to outdo Dubai on this last point. To optimize its military aura, the city needs to make a success of its world arms fair, in other words, to make it the absolute reference in the field, with the complicity of some of the world's biggest arms dealers, such as the United States, France and Great Britain[12].

Created in 1993 in Abu Dhabi, well before the explosive economic development of Dubai in the 2000s, the IDEX exhibition seems to reveal the military tropism of the great man of Abu Dhabi at the time, who was also Minister of Defense and Deputy Prime Minister: Mohamed ben Zayed. Better still, this exhibition reflects a will to power that is certainly not innocent in the context of the second Gulf War. After the invasion of Kuwait by Iraq, all the countries of the Gulf Cooperation Council became aware that they had to strengthen their defense capabilities. Saudi Arabia, Kuwait, Oman, Bahrain and the UAE therefore purchased huge quantities of weapons.

As chief of staff, MBZ is advancing his plans. Under his leadership, Abu Dhabi is becoming an airport, port, military

---

12. https://www.amnesty.fr/controle-des-armes/actualites/les-cinq-plus-grands-marchands-darmes-mondiaux

4. From arming to land grabbing

and commercial hub. For the tactician, linking the military and the economic is the best way to reduce the influence of the other more discreet Emirates, and to gain the upper hand over Dubai, notably thanks to the OFFSET program, set up at the end of the 1980s. The project: that defense contracts be accompanied by a concentrated investment in the economy of the Emirate of Abu Dhabi. As an expert from the Middle East Policy Council details, the UAE offset program was created as a result of the modernization of the armed forces. This required the acquisition of sophisticated defense systems with limited manpower. The considerable funding required for the purchase of modern weapons systems posed a dilemma for policymakers: should defence spending be undertaken at the expense of national wealth redistribution and development?

The UAE offset program was therefore designed to take advantage of the fierce competition within the defense industry to achieve both goals, to restructure its military and to implement an offset program consistent with the government's overall economic strategy. This strategy utilizes the UAE's positive attributes - its geographic location, infrastructure, liquid capital markets and vast oil and gas reserves - to redistribute wealth to UAE citizens, create value for the economy, enhance competitiveness and encourage strategic trade. The compensation obligation for foreign suppliers is set at 60% of the purchase contract value.

Large corporations are quickly running into difficulties. The OFFSET program encourages multinational companies to seek out business opportunities and local private sector partners in areas ranging from technology services to health care to solar energy to shipbuilding. As a result, a consistent "deal flow" of several hundred projects has been created. A knowledgeable source at the time, who worked on behalf of the Emiratis, recently told us on condition of anonymity:

the 60% compensation on tens of billions of annual arms purchases was to go to Abu Dhabi; but how to inject so much money? All the major arms manufacturers had to set up special offices with the recruitment of engineers, investment and financial specialists, and dedicated *project managers* who struggled to find development projects to finance in order to drain the excessive financial flows. Dassault and Boeing, to name but a few, soon found themselves short of projects.

Unlike Dubai, which had a development strategy, Abu Dhabi developed in a rush, in excess and in the imperative need to spend *cash* to build. Strange as it may seem, attempts by some of the authorities' experts and close advisors at the time to extend the law to other emirates failed because of MBZ's determination to make Abu Dhabi the new Dubai.

We no longer knew what to do, what to spend, what projects to propose. We had oil but fewer and fewer ideas. Groups that could not find projects good enough

4. From arming to land grabbing

to absorb so many billions and continued to sell arms to Abu Dhabi sometimes even preferred to break the rule and face penalties and fines. Countries like the United States, France, Germany and Britain found themselves in a very critical position in the 2010s and feared only that they would end up in litigation and court cases with the UAE, one of their best customers at the time.

Critics can't help it: MBZ is determined to use arms purchases to consolidate its power over its emirate. Hence the raïs' deep desire to increase the UAE's geopolitical influence, notably *through the* creation of the ECSSR, the Emirates Center for Strategic and Security Studies, which the security obsession will end up corrupting. However, MBZ's development of Abu Dhabi was based on an early commitment to ecology, convinced of the growing importance of the "green economy" as fossil fuels became increasingly scarce.

Since 2009, Abu Dhabi has been investing in the fields of ecovillages, green public transport, green buildings, reducing the number of cars on the road, new standards for greening real estate construction, etc.[13] The heart of the project is *business.* As proof, ten years later, the emirate has become a specialist in *land grabbing in* order to get its hands on the rare metals that are essential to the green economy. To the point of raising concerns, which were echoed by *Le Point:*

---

13. https://www.lemonde.fr/planete/article/2009/06/03/comment-abu-dhabi-va-devenir-une-ville-durable_1201682_3244.html

Are numerous Chinese and Emirati companies despoiling the land-based mineral resources of some African countries with impunity? In a report on April 24, 2019, Reuters claims that billions of dollars worth of gold and other mineral resources are being smuggled out of Africa to the United Arab Emirates and China.

The British news agency goes further, claiming that this particularly lucrative, though perfectly illegal, trade would fuel certain conflicts - including the one that has killed tens of thousands of Yemenis since 2015. It would violate human rights and endanger the environment of the countries in which these resources are extracted in total disregard of international trade rules and international law.[14]

Thus appear some slippery aspects of the development of a liberal island towards an expansionist, authoritarian, militarized country, ready to do anything to conquer the world. The State, modest, is not exempt from crises or disillusionment; however, it develops militarily and economically, to evolve little by little towards a predatory regime in the name of its integrity and survival, evoking to the specialists various historical models like

- Sparta, one of the most powerful empire-cities of the Greek empire, marked, like the Emirates by the

---

14. https://www.lepoint.fr/afrique/or-diamants-terres-rares-la-ruee-pre-datrice-vers-l-afrique-08-08-2019-2328983_3826.php

confiscation of the power by a minority, and by a very clear inclination for the military thing; and

   - Venice, whose UAE is similar in the comparable importance of religion, trade and armaments in its development.

From now on, for the Emirates, the Emirates are not enough: their economic, military and political development has whetted their appetite enough for them to consider conquering the world - specifically the Arab world, in the first instance.

5. From emissary to ally

In 2019, Mohamed bin Zayed is inducted as one of the 100 most influential people in the world. He is also probably one of the richest people on the planet thanks to the Abu Dhabi sovereign wealth fund. His importance has grown in parallel with that of the Emirates. Nothing of what has become of the Federation in the last twenty years is totally foreign to Mohamed ben Zayed; and, in the last five years, his choice of authoritarianism has reinforced his status. For Armin Arefi, a journalist at Le *Point*, MBZ is "the new leader of the Middle East". Indeed, "Crown Prince Mohammed bin Zayed, alias MBZ, a strong man and privileged interlocutor of the White House, is reshaping the Arab world."[15] He has been able to get the ear of the United States during Donald Trump's time, and he is very close to his Saudi ally. The United States, Saudi Arabia and the United Arab Emirates are united on at least

___

15. https://www.lepoint.fr/monde/emirats-mbz-nouveau-chef-du-moyen-orient-20-09-2019-2336823_24.php

three issues fundamental to the world in general and the Arab world in particular:

- Iran,

- the Muslim Brotherhood, and

- the Israeli-Palestinian question.

Like Nasser, Saddam Hussein and Muammar Gaddafi, MBZ sees the Arab world through the eyes of the military man that he is. The son of Zayed Ben Sultan Al Nahyane, founder of the UAE, MBZ has been swimming in the deep waters of UAE politics for a very long time. Quickly turning to international affairs, he was noticed by the Americans at the time of Iraq's invasion of Kuwait in August 1990, when he went to Washington to negotiate a massive arms purchase as Abu Dhabi's defense minister and deputy commander-in-chief of the UAE's then-weak armed forces. The young MBZ, trained as a helicopter pilot by the British at the Royal Military Academy in Sandhurst, won over his interlocutors.

The Pentagon, seeking to cultivate accommodating allies in the Gulf, had seen in him a promising partner. The favourite son of the nearly illiterate Bedouin who founded the United Arab Emirates, Mohammed bin Zayed was a serious guy, a British-trained helicopter pilot who had persuaded his father to transfer $4 billion to the U.S. Treasury to help pay for the 1991 Iraq war. Richard A. Clarke, then Deputy Secretary of State, reassured members that the young prince "is not and never will be a threat to stability or peace in the region," he testified before Congress. It is unimaginable. I would even say that his country is working for peace."[16]

The man thus seems a sure ally for Washington, to the point of being able to demand, as early as 2001, that the White House bomb the Afghan headquarters of the Al Jazeera channel before the invasion of Afghanistan, in order to put an end to what he considers Qatari disinformation - this is one of the discoveries made possible in 2017 by the Wikileaks. The request was followed up in Kabul, in November 2001, and seems to have been renewed in 2003 with the media's Iraqi offices. Unquestionably, MBZ knows how to build his network by relying on his charisma and on the stability of his country, which he presents as the main agent in the fight against terrorism in the Middle East. He has received a plethora of decorations all over the world, probably for good and loyal services rendered, always in the name of the general interest... Thus, in Germany he has been awarded the Grand Cross of the Order of Merit of the FRG, in Spain the Grand Cordon of the Order of Civil Merit, in France the Grand Cross of the National Order of Merit; other distinctions have been awarded to him in South Korea, Jordan, Kosovo, Kuwait, Malaysia, Morocco, and Palestine; finally, in the United Kingdom, this obviously

---

16. https://www.nytimes.com/2019/06/02/world/middleeast/crown-prince-mohammed-bin-zayed.html, article on June 20, 2019

exceptional man has been made a Knight of the Grand Cross of the Order of St. Michael and of St. George.

Yet he had to wait until he was 53 years old to have his moment of glory. In 2014, he became the country's crown prince. It is a troubled time. MBZ needs to strengthen its alliances across the Atlantic as quickly as possible to consolidate its federation despite the tremors felt after the Arab Spring. We must hurry. Barack Obama has announced his desire to withdraw gradually from the region. Saudi Arabia is in trouble because of the fall in the price of a barrel of crude oil. If the American president carries out his promise, MBZ has a boulevard to impose the UAE as the preferred local interlocutor of the North American giant.

Proactive, the Emir is also cunning: sensing the wind turning in favor of the candidate Donald Trump, he tries to impose himself, taking with him his protégé, the young Mohamed ben Salmane of Saudi Arabia. Several secret meetings took place between MBZ's relatives and Donald Trump's campaign team. He is the buffer between the old post-Obama world and the new one that will take shape with whoever becomes the next American president. Who of all the Arab leaders of weight, apart from MBZ, can boast so many years of experience, to be still there since 2011 despite the situation, and to be the one to count on for this new Arab world under construction? No one.

So, through secret meetings with Donald Trump Jr and American, Lebanese and Israeli businessmen, the Emir is placing his pawns with one objective, according to the analysis of Majed Al Ansari, a Qatari researcher:

Saudi Arabia and the UAE thought they could buy the US administration in the long run. Kushner and Trump could be sensitive to this because they were already doing business in the Quartet countries as well as in Qatar. Unlike Qatar, which did not want to enter this unhealthy game, Riyadh and Abu Dhabi only scored points in the short term. This is also due to the specificity of the American administration and the powers of the President of the United States: he can dismiss one of his advisers within the hour if he no longer likes him. After Steve Bannon and Michael Cohen were removed, the pressure on Qatar has largely diminished on his part. This is proof that these two advisors were acting on behalf of the interests of Saudi Arabia and the UAE.

Cabbales, pressure and anti-Qatar lobbying are multiplying with a triple objective:
- Sanctuarize the influence of the UAA in the arena of power,
- limit the Islamist threat posed by the Muslim Brotherhood, and
- contain the democratic inclination that Abu Dhabi does not look favorably upon.

5. From emissary to ally

Washington is not fooled, but it has not lost sight of its own obvious interest, which consists of controlling its main ally in the region in order to ensure the stability of an area that is still in turmoil. Disappointment for the Americans: very quickly, MBZ began to take liberties with the American line by relying on its ally and protégé, Mohamed ben Salmane.

6. From alliance to blockade

Mohamed bin Salmane is the anti-terrorist asset that Mohamed bin Zayed manages to impose on the White House at the expense of the former favorite dismissed in June 2017, Mohamed bin Nayef bin Abdulaziz Al Saud. MBN had been America's man since the attacks of September 11, 2001, and the launch of George W. Bush's fight against terrorism. But his fate was tied up on January 23, 2015, when King Abdullah bin Abdulaziz Al Saud died. Salman bin Abdulaziz Al Saud, his half-brother, acceded to the throne. Mohammed ben Salmane is 29 years old. He is a minister, advisor to his father... and unknown in Washington. Nevertheless, thanks to the king's support, he has been able to wear a number of remarkably diverse hats in record time - head of the royal cabinet, minister of defense, chairman of a council for economic affairs and development... - hence his nickname of Mister Everything. After ousting two competitors, including MBN, the U.S. anti-terrorist ally, officially for health reasons, he became crown prince.

In reality, this rise owes much to MBZ, who promoted MBS in Washington early on. In January 2017, a month before Trump's inauguration, MBZ secretly flew to New York. He did not inform outgoing U.S. President Barack Obama, whose aides only learned of his arrival when MBZ's name was discovered on a flight manifest. According to an article in the *Washington Post*[17], MBZ met with Donald Trump's inner circle of advisors[18], namely Michael Flynn, the short-lived national security adviser who was forced to resign on February 13, 2017 for his suspicious ties to Moscow, Jared Kushner, the president's son-in-law and special adviser with whom MBZ has had a close relationship ever since, and his "ideologue" Stephen Bannon as for him sidelined on August 18, 2017. MBZ's main objective was to offer his mediation to the Trump family. MBZ's brother, the national security adviser of the United Arab Emirates, had arranged a meeting in the Seychelles between Erik Prince, the founder of Blackwater, and a Russian close to Vladimir Putin. The idea was to establish a parallel line of communication between Moscow and President-elect Donald Trump, according to the *Washington Post*. But this meeting would also have made MBZ the man to solve the problems in the Gulf for Trump.

---

17. https://www.washingtonpost.com/world/national-security/blackwater-founder-held-secret-seychelles-meeting-to-establish-trump-putin-back-channel/2017/04/03/95908a08-1648-11e7-ada0-1489b735b3a3_story.html
18. http://www.middleeasteye.net/fr/opinions/coup-Page80d-tat-royal-en-arabie-saoudite-la-suite-173511407

On March 14, 2017, at the White House, Donald Trump, who has supported his rise, met with an MBS who has been portrayed for several months as an impatient reformer by Bloomberg[19] and *The Economist*[20]. "We've put our man on top,"[21], Trump reportedly told friends in June 2017, when Prince Mohammed bin Nayef was ousted as crown prince in favor of Mohammed bin Salmane[22], satisfying Abu Dhabi and Washington.

In this context, it is easy to understand why Donald Trump is devoting his first official trip to Saudi Arabia to affirm three objectives:
- strengthen the relationship with this country,
- sign contracts worth one hundred and ten billion dollars, and
- to isolate more firmly Iran, considered as "terrorist".

A fruitful meeting for the two allies who, according to some experts, did not care about the risk of conflict of interest brought by a businessman turned politician! However, this rapprochement between Saudi Arabia and the United States also sealed the rapprochement between Saudi Arabia and the UAE. This pas-de-deux between neighbors really began

19. https://www.bloomberg.com/news/articles/2016-04-04/saudi-arabia-s-deputy-crown-prince-outlines-plans-transcript
20. https://www.economist.com/middle-east-and-africa/2016/01/06/transcript-interview-with-muhammad-bin-salman
21. Michael Wolff, *Fire and Fury: Inside the Trump White House* (New York: Henry Holt and Company, 2018).
22. https://www.aljazeera.com/news/2018/01/put-man-top-trump-mbs-book-claims-180105124054629.html

when Nasser's Egypt expelled the Muslim Brotherhood from its country. The members of this brotherhood took refuge in the Gulf countries. At that time, the Gulf countries lacked experts in two sectors: education and justice, specialties of the Brotherhood. The latter shaped both sectors throughout the region. Sometimes, the marriage between Wahhabism and the Muslim Brotherhood has produced other variants. This is the case of the Sahwa ("awakening") currents, which oscillate between conservatism and politics. On the moral level, its militants advocate purification; on the political level, they try to influence political regimes and constitutions towards greater rigorism.

In August 1990, the invasion of Kuwait by Iraq created a wave of panic. The Muslim Brotherhood gave their support to Saddam Hussein. Riyadh saw this support as a betrayal, but its attitude was torn by the need to preserve their alliance with the Brotherhood in the name of stability in Yemen. As a pragmatic policy, Saudi Arabia is able to ally itself with groups that it considers useful, even with the shiite Zaydis. During the Dhofar war of 1964-1976, the country made a pact with the communists! By dint of compromise in the name of realism, the Saudis avoid being very careful about the ideology of their partners.

Conversely, for Abu Dhabi, the Muslim Brotherhood is a fundamental problem. The Brotherhood threatens the unity of the confederation. Indeed, in the north, thanks to the very conservative Islah party, it is growing among 60% of the population. Worse, the majority of the military is from this region. In addition to this internal threat, there is an external threat because the Muslim Brotherhood does not lack support. In short, MBZ fears a coup. His alliance with Saudi Arabia aims to create a common front between enemies of the Brotherhood, which he considers even more threatening than Iran. But, in the balance, MBZ fears the Brotherhood more than Iran. Thus, a game of three-cornered billiards is being played with Qatar, where many Muslim Brothers have taken refuge to escape Saudi Arabia's hostile attitude towards them. As Haouas Taguia, a researcher at the Al Jazeera Center Studies, explained to me during an interview in October 2019,

> Doha wanted to be independent of Saudi ideology because it did not agree with its policy and welcomed preachers driven out by Riyadh, such as Youssef Qaradawi, the leading intellectual of the Brotherhood at the time, arrived in Doha. He was banned from Egypt and the UAE, but for a time he became the reference point for opponents of the Wahhabi and Salafist ideology of its big neighbor. The Arab Spring then put in the public square the state of relations of these three countries with Islamism and fundamentalism. Thus, for a time, the Brotherhood was used as a scapegoat for all the misfortunes of the region.

From then on, the situation changed for the benefit of the UAE. The borders are porous to the Brotherhood's danger,

6. From alliance to blockade

sailing between Tunisia, Egypt, Libya, Syria and, therefore, the UAE and Saudi Arabia. A double strategic option is needed: on the one hand, to develop a consensus around the assimilation of the Brotherhood to a terrorist entity; on the other hand, to trigger an external conflict in order to defuse the internal danger. In this perspective, one of the greatest diplomatic and political coups of MBZ, and his Saudi ally MBS, occurs on June 5, 2017 within the Gulf itself with the total isolation of Qatar.

7. From turnaround to grain of sand

The brutal launching of the land, air and sea blockade is a new affront to international regulations. However, the alliance with the United States is at work. Mohamed ben Zayed obtained the support of the Americans and many Western countries to impose his authoritarian model in the face of Middle Eastern chaos and fears of terrorism. Doha's status is changing. From being an ally, it became the enemy because it prevented MBZ, erected as a hero of stability, from conquering the Arab world. It is a reversal. As Olivier Da Lage, a journalist at RFI, summarizes it,

> in fact, there was no real falling out between the uae and Qatar, apart from the usual pre-eminence disputes that led to the withdrawal of Qatar and Bahrain from the uae federation project, which eventually came to fruition without these two emirates, as they preferred to become full-fledged states. Nor was there any particular falling out at the time between Saudi Arabia and Qatar,

by far the closest Gulf country to Riyadh, if only because both are predominantly Wahhabi. The division of the Gulf Cooperation Council along the fault line that came to light in 2017 was therefore definitely not written into the conditions of the UAE's birth.

The outbreak of the 2017 crisis refers less to a predictable diplomatic hiccup than to a quarrel of people and interests. Accusing Qatar of harboring regional terrorism and considering Doha as Tehran's best partner are mere pretexts. Undermining Qatar allows MBZ to take on a rival power head-on; and it allows the Trump clan to settle big money stories. Indeed, in April 2017, Jared Kushner, Donald Trump's special adviser and son-in-law, met with Ali Shareef Al Emadi, Qatar's finance minister, to negotiate the bailout of a Trumpian building at 666 5e Avenue in New York. Since it was bought for nearly 2 billion dollars in 2008, it had turned out to be a money pit. It is likely that the Qatari minister's refusal to put his hand in the wallet will seal the fate of Doha[23].

On June 6, 2017, Saudi Arabia, the UAE, Egypt, and Bahrain decided to isolate Qatar from the regional and international scene. Their three main demands:

- to end alleged support for terrorism,

- cut its ties with Iran and

- turn off the Al Jazeera channel.

___

23. https://theintercept.com/2018/03/02/jared-kushner-real-estate-qatar-blockade/ and developed in the French version www.huffpostmaghreb.com/2018/03/03/represailles-de-jared-kus_n_19363596.html

It does not matter that there is no evidence of support for terrorism or Iranian ideology. These pious lies mask the real motivations of this terrible coup de force. Indeed, how to survive when the only land border one has is with Saudi Arabia? How to maintain air traffic in a geopolitical pocketbook when the space of its neighbors is forbidden? How to reunite mixed families divided by the blockade? How to continue the preparation of the 2022 World Cup? The UAE and its allies have a simple answer: if Qatar abdicates its sovereignty, the blockade will disappear. But to the dismay of MBZ and MBS, Doha is holding its ground and counter-attacking by dismantling unfounded allegations and knowingly false accusations, by multiplying the revelations on the obscure maneuvers of Riyadh and Abu Dhabi in Washington, by pointing out that the Saudi and Emirati economies are also impacted by the blockade, by pointing to the social and political changes that are undermining the stability of Saudi Arabia and generating instability, and by strengthening its positions in Yemen, which is costing Riyadh dearly.

Another grain of sand also disrupts the blockade: the families of the Gulf are split on both sides of artificial borders. Therefore, punishing one's neighbor is also punishing oneself. When the blockade began, many families whose members worked in Saudi Arabia, the Emirates, Bahrain or Egypt were separated overnight. There are also many families by marriage between these small countries: three out of four Qataris have a close family member from one of the countries responsible for the blockade. Many students have found themselves in extremely delicate situations, expelled overnight from Saudi Arabia or the Emirates. Many Qataris who were in Mecca when the crisis broke out were also expelled from the country. Many patients treated in hospitals in Saudi Arabia were asked to leave the country. Finally, the desire to censor Al Jazeera did not improve the Emirates' image.

Supported by the United Nations, which declared the blockade illegal, Doha, in the name of its violated sovereignty, turned to an army of lawyers and legal advisors to defend its integrity, and to demand freedom of movement, transportation, education and worship. With success: two years after the savage operation, when you walk around the capital of Qatar, the consequences of the blockade are no longer visible. Whether in the developing neighborhoods or on the construction sites of the buildings in West Bay and on the Corniche, business is booming. The new national museum, signed by Jean Nouvel, has opened its doors in spring 2019; the Wakif souk, the social epicenter of the city, does not empty in the evening; the prestigious hotels that welcome many tourists, even during Ramadan, have not seen a reduction in their international clientele; the new Hamad International Airport, a regional *hub*, is operating at full capacity; Qatar Airways announced record orders for aircraft in December 2017; preparations for the 2022 soccer World Cup, the first to be held in the Arab world, are continuing despite controversy, and construction of the seven stadiums is progressing well.

Another example: on the education front, the hobbyhorse of former Emir Hamad's wife, Sheikha Moza, the Qatar Foundation (dedicated to youth-related programs) continues to expand its projects around the world and, through the Education above all program, is providing literacy and schooling to children who would never have been literate in their own countries. In May 2018, the NGO Silatech promised one million jobs for youth in the Arab world in the near future, and the immediate creation of 200,000 jobs for youth in Morocco alone. Enough to keep competing with the UAE on their own turf!

In sum, MBZ's strategy is failing miserably. In Yemen, the dream of stabilization has been slipping away since March 2015, as a humanitarian crisis of terrifying proportions follows the massacres. Qatar has risen, albeit weakened. On the other hand, MBZ has won in one respect: the Gulf Cooperation Council has disappeared. It was the only body that could calm its ardor, since Qatar was part of it. A small victory, no doubt, for the one that the Arab Spring had already panicked in 2011...

8. From the springs to the diplomatic offensive

In 2011, the protests that shook several countries, from the Maghreb to the Mashreq, triggered a wave of panic in the United States. They see the hand of the Muslim Brotherhood. Thirty years of authoritarianism and dictatorships have created pockets of poverty on which Islamist movements have flourished. Through charity organizations and entry strategies, the Muslim Brotherhood has become a serious counter-power that is logically biding its time.

From Tunisia to Egypt, through Morocco, Libya, Syria and Bahrain, people are demonstrating against dictatorships, nepotism, the absence of free elections and fundamental rights, which are all the less acceptable since the economic and social crisis in the region has been worsening for years since the 2008 global crisis. Indeed, Western countries are the main economic and commercial partners of the MENA zone

(Middle East North Africa); the Maghreb as well as the Middle East are also impacted by the difficult economic situation.

After rising up against colonialism in the 1950s and 1960s, young people in their own countries are revolting against their authoritarian powers with demands for their individual freedoms and against socio-economic inequalities, in a process that we described with Azouz Begag[24]. The more young people seek to improve their quality of life, the greater the political instability and the risk of violence. As early as 2007, Emmanuel Todd and Youssef Courbage described this pressure for sociological reasons: the very rapid demographic transition in part of the Arab world has, as in other regions of the world, provoked social violence[25]. The memory of the massacres in Algiers, where the army killed five hundred young people during a demonstration in 1988, prolonging the tremors of the Berber Spring of 1980, remains vivid. This bloody episode marked the beginning of Algeria's "black decade," which resulted in hundreds of thousands of victims.

There is nothing ephemeral about these upheavals: the barbarities committed by the government and its military affiliates have deeply affected young Algerians, just as their peers were traumatized in Iraq, Syria, Lebanon or the Gaza Strip. Yet no particular attention has been paid by national or international political bodies to the collateral damage caused to children. Since 2016, the popular uprisings agitating the Rif

24. *Letter to the Arab Youth*, Erick Bonnier, 2018.
25. *Le Rendez-vous des civilisations*, Le Seuil, 2007.

region with Hirak ("the movement") are symptomatic of social and political instability. The Moroccan protests were sparked in Al-Hoceima on the day Mouhcine Fikri, a young fish seller, was killed by a dumpster after being arrested with an illegal shipment of swordfish. In a landlocked and politically marginalized region, suffering from high unemployment, this death had provoked major demonstrations, similar to those of Sidi Bouzid in 2010, when the immolation of a young street vendor had set Tunisia ablaze.

A year later, the first young Rifans were sentenced to heavy prison terms, while the king dismissed three ministers in order to reassure his young subjects without calling everything into question. There are still structural problems: unemployment among young Moroccans is as high as 40 per cent; the informal sector - especially in the Rif region, cannabiculture - is considered the main source of employment; and seven out of ten young people have no qualifications. For many young people in this vast area, whether Moroccans, Tunisians, Algerians or Egyptians, the rural exodus and then exile to Europe seem to be the only alternative for a decent future. Faced with the disarray of the population, the Islamist political parties tried to pass for the ideal alternative. Their retrograde projects in terms of freedoms and human rights were less appealing than an objective reality: no other structured political force was credibly positioned. Many of these parties were linked to the Muslim Brotherhood.

In Libya and Syria, two wars exploded in 2011, revealing powers on the brink of collapse. In 2011, the regime of

8. From the springs to the diplomatic offensive

Muammar Gaddafi is overthrown, leaving room for merciless battles between

- government forces recognized by the United Nations,
- political forces of Marshal Haftar supported by France and the UAE, among others, and
- jihadist currents, including the EI, which created the third capital of the Caliphate in Sirte.

In Syria, the struggles are no less bloody between

- the regime of Bashar Al Assad,
- the Syrian democratic forces,
- the armed jihadist opposition, and
- Islamic State, which emerged in Syria and Iraq in July 2014 under the leadership of the self-proclaimed caliph Al Baghdadi.

The Islamic State claims between 40,000 and 80,000 fighters, including more than 30,000 foreigners from over 100 countries.

Revolts and wars would be enough to worry the UAE, but in addition to this polymorphous powder keg, there is the unrest in the Gulf. This began in Bahrain, with the revolts in Manama's Pearl Square in 2011. They were quickly put down by Saudi Arabia, with the support of the UAE, which considers the peninsula as a satellite. No matter! Everywhere, MBZ fears the two elements that could eventually weaken its power:

- the emergence of a real democratic demand; and
- the rise of Islamist counterpowers as embodied by the Muslim Brotherhood.

The results, it is true, are not the most reassuring.

In Morocco, following the failure of the February 2011 demonstrations, the Islamists of the Justice and Development party came to power.

In Algeria, things are less advanced: no "Algerian spring" - it will be necessary to wait until 2019 for the beginning of a change!

In Tunisia, after the adoption of a new constitution, elections were held and led to the rise of the Islamist party Ennahda, the country's largest party in 2018.

Egypt is the scene of the worst revolutionary failure: the Tahrir Square revolution certainly got the better of Hosni Mubarak's regime; but the 2013 elections brought Mohamed Morsi and the rigorous and autocratic Muslim Brotherhood to power.

On the Syrian side, faced with Daech, the international coalition led by the United States, Saudi Arabia, the United Arab Emirates and Qatar in particular, is not skimping on any bombing to fight the jihadists on the ground, soliciting the support of the YPG, the Syrian Kurds, in this perspective.

Since the 2003 invasion, Iraq has been torn between
- the Shiites, who are in the majority demographically and were brought to power by the White House after the over-throw of Saddam Hussein,
- the "de-Baathification" of the country,
- the Sunnis, who are badly treated, and
- Daech which threatens the country's very fragile stability.

In Yemen, President Saleh, an ally of the United States, Saudi Arabia and the United States of America, has had to flee. The Houthis took advantage of this to go on the offensive

8. From the springs to the diplomatic offensive

and seize the capital, Sana'a, and the port of Aden, which Abu Dhabi and Riyadh consider an existential threat to the Arabian Peninsula, the Gulf, and the Strait of Hormuz.

Everywhere in the region, attacks are multiplying; and the news from Iran is not more favorable to MBZ. It is against this backdrop that US President Barack Obama pokes his nose into negotiating an Iranian nuclear deal finally signed in July 2015. Saudi Arabia and the UAE are seeing red. For them, this agreement is a first step that risks marking Tehran's return to the concert of nations. Mohamed ben Zayed understands that, in order not to lose his power and influence, he must urgently put things in order and go on the diplomatic or even military offensive thanks to these famous tools of *hard* and *soft powers* put in place for years, along four lines:

- to finish extinguishing the Arab Spring,
- to consider without complex each interference which would seem useful,
- consolidate ties with Saudi Arabia and, especially, the United States, and
- not skimping on noble anti-terrorist arguments likely to seduce Western allies, for example by equating democratic aspirations with Islamism to the tune of: "You see? Wherever there has been democratization, Islamists have moved in."

The United Arab Emirates intend to take advantage of the chaos to advance their pawns; and MBZ has some very concrete ideas to achieve this...

9. From Ennahda to Sissi

The Tunisian case is unique. Although the country is on the brink of collapse, with very limited resources, it has stabilized and begun its democratic transition with a new Constitution and elections in late 2019... which have consecrated the importance of Ennahda, the Muslim Brotherhood party. However, the Gulf countries have largely invested in the country since the Arab Spring, in order to accompany it or try to destabilize it. The UAE's game is murky. It consists of short-circuiting Qatar's initiatives in favour of the democratic process, notably by denouncing Doha's support for the Ennahda party, which Abu Dhabi has not managed to remove[26].

Hence small retaliatory measures that speak volumes. Thus, on December 19, 2017, the Tunisian president called for local elections. MBZ is furious, because the context seems to him favorable to Ennahda. As a punishment, from December

---

26. https://orientxxi.info/magazine/la-tunisie-un-champ-d-affrontement-entre-les-pays-du-golfe,2387

26, Tunisian women are no longer allowed to take Emirates planes. Immediately, Tunisia closed its airports to all flights of the company... temporarily, because the financial consequences were not reasonable for the country. In reality, in this game of influence and alliances, the judge of peace could be the economic situation of Tunisia. The sirens of the highest bidder should be irresistible, but they will have to deal with the ambition of Ennahda. In 2019, the party is demanding the appointment of a prime minister from within its political formation - refused. Nevertheless, MBZ would have launched, in June 2020, rumors of a coup d'état relayed by the Turkish intelligence agency and several European media - in vain. The struggle continues, in Carthage as elsewhere.

Thus, in Algeria, after several months of "hirak", the country obtained its second independence. After the events of 1962, the Algerian population succeeded in freeing itself from its leader, who had been in power for 20 years. Less than two weeks after a presidential election that brought former Prime Minister Abdelmadjdid Tebboune to the head of state, Ahmed Gaïd Salah, 84, a pillar of the Algerian regime, surrendered on the night of December 22, 2019. In power for decades, he was until then the main brake on a constructive evolution of democracy in the country that let the Hirak reach its ends.

The scenario was neither envisaged by the Algerians, nor anticipated by MBZ, with whom he was in constant contact. For a long time, Algeria had been protected from democratic outbursts. In the name of the security imperative brandished by the government, it had been repeated over and over that there had already been an "Algerian Spring" in October 1988, and that the consequences had been tragic. Indeed, the opening to a multi-party system had accelerated the arrival of the islamists, who were deprived of their victory in 1992, leading to a terrible decade for the country. This rhetoric allowed the Bouteflika clan to plunder the country for a long time. Gaïd Salah was the guarantor of a certain continuity and a small evolution, despite his history, his age and his inadequacy with the aspirations expressed in the ballot box by the Algerians. The UAE and Saudi Arabia know that they are facing the largest country in Africa, in the most favourable geostrategic position in relation to the Algerian people.

- to Europe,

- in the Sahel and

- to sub-Saharan Africa, whose resources excite appetites.

The U.S. is faced with a twofold problem: on the one hand, MBZ is not a staunch supporter of democracy; on the other hand, in the Arab world, democracy seems to bring to power the enemies of democracy, in this case the Islamist parties. At least they still hope to remake themselves in Libya. There, they think they have the solution. Yet the overthrow of Muammar Gaddafi has not resolved anything in eight years of conflict. To the credit of the Emirates, no one else has found a solution to date. The war, like the clan and government struggle between Tripoli and Benghazi, is never-ending. The international community pretends to manage the unmanageable, *id is* the intrusion of all into a political story that should be settled by Libyans first and last... but the worst is elsewhere.

Revelations by the BBC about war crimes committed by Abu Dhabi in Libya[27], after cases of torture two years ago in Emirati prisons in Yemen, have not finished causing a stir. Behind the Emirati support for a new Libya in its own image, there is one man: the inconvenient Marshal Khalifa Haftar. He had been accused for months of war crimes in the city of Derna, while fighting was still raging in the country's capital. Since April 4, 2019, the government of national unity led by Fayez el Sarraj, recognized by the United Nations, is threatened every day by the one who is none other than the hand of the Emirates in Western Libya. In the capital, displaced Libyans number in the tens of thousands... while MBZ was delivering a new boatload of weapons to Haftar across the Egyptian border

And we are not at the end of our surprises since half of the funds of the former raïs would have arrived in Abu Dhabi for a long time and the second half would have been forwarded there at the end of 2019[28]. In November 2019, Haftar's foreign minister, Abdulhadi Lahouij, at a conference in Brussels, was confident despite the apocalyptic situation there in terms of human rights.

We do not have many allies to help us out of this crisis, while with 21 million weapons in circulation,

---

27. https://www.bbc.com/news/av/world-africa-48105968/libya-war-crimes-videos-shared-on-social-media
28. https://www.francetvinfo.fr/monde/afrique/libye/ou-sont-passes-les-milliards-libyens-disparus_3056373.html

the threat is also valid for Africa, the Arab world and Europe. Among the states that support the jihadists and militias in Tripoli, Qatar is a full player. Our support from the United Arab Emirates is aimed above all at the Libya of the future, a Libya that is secure and peaceful, where there will be no more rapes, violence, prisons or summary executions. We control 90% of the territory, so, recognized or not, we want to start there, compared to Sarraj who has not applied anything, and in particular with the Abu Dhabi agreement on the disarmament of the militias.

The forces are sizing each other up. The struggle for power pits the national unity government, backed by Turkey and Qatar, against haftar's forces, supported by Russia, the uae and Emmanuel Macron's France. Boosted by this support, haftar's forces have called on madkhali salafist groups, even if it means overestimating these affiliates. The madkhalis are neither choirboys nor the freedom fighters and secularists that Paris describes. Originating from Saudi Arabia, they are quietist salafists, that is to say proselytizing and submissive Muslims. Proselytes, because they want to convince the population to practice a rigorous and demanding Islam; submissive, because they want all their energy to be spent on religion - which leads them to abandon politics.

Their leader is Rabbi El Madkhali. Born in 1931, he emerged in Saudi Arabia during the Gulf War. Since then, Riyadh has

9. From Ennahda to Sissi

supported him because he professes that any rebellion to authority is *haram*. The Madkhali faithful will never call for opposition to the political leader on whom they depend territorially. On the other hand, they will always be willing, in return for payment, to destroy temples and shrines where the traditionally peaceful Sufis pray.

Egypt comes from a different logic. For MBZ, all the political planets seem to be aligned:
- a finished revolution,
- stifled democratic aspirations,
- a fierce military regime and
- absolute support of Marshal Sissi to his Emirati sponsor.

The Muslim Brotherhood's rise to power in Egypt caused concern in the United States, Israel and the Emirates; but Mohamed Morsi's Brotherhood presidency, which began in June 2012, ended in July 2013, when a counter-revolution endorsed a return to the established order, embodied by Marshal Abdelfattah Sissi. Now, Mohammed bin Zayed and Mohammed bin Salmane dream of duplicating this model of counter-revolution in Algeria and Sudan.

Especially since the relationship between Cairo and Abu Dhabi is solid and longstanding. The country's resources, which are generally stretched to the limit, are linked to the colossal revenues of the Suez Canal and, above all, to external support. Since 1978, the United States has been buying peace with Israel; and MBZ itself does not skimp on the small gifts that keep relations good. On April 25, 2016, he announced an

United Arab Emirates conquering the world

exceptional 4 billion in funding for the Egyptian economy. On November 14, 2019, this funding was complemented by a joint investment financing plan of twenty billion dollars. In exchange, Sissi promises to help the Gulf if there is a war.

In reality, the Egyptian military regime suits several regional players, starting with the new partner of the Saudis and the Emiratis. Sinai is a powder keg; and the peninsula is safer since the arrival of Sissi. MBZ can only be satisfied with this, especially since the Muslim Brotherhood has been banished from Egypt. However, this satisfaction remains limited, so it pushes the eau to seek new development relays.

10. From Sudan to Berbera

On December 19, 2018, Sudan is rocked by protests driven by increasingly difficult access to basic necessities. Eight months of protests lead the army to overthrow Omar El Bechir who had ruled for three decades. At one time supported by the Islamists, the man is accused of crimes against humanity in the Darfur genocide and is wanted by the International Criminal Court. In his country, he is accused of widespread corruption. Small potatoes for MBZ, who expects to maintain his former influence in Sudan!

General Abdelfattah Al Buhrane, who was heading the Transitional Military Council at the time, reassured him that he wanted to maintain privileged relations with Saudi Arabia and the UAE. What does it matter if this Al Buhrane commanded the Sudanese ground forces, hostile to Abu Dhabi, deployed in Yemen? Pragmatism is required. MBZ wants to keep its grip; and, for its part, Sudan needs cash and liquidity, as was customary: to limit the protest, wasn't the UAE reputed to have paid, in January 2019, "according to a Sudanese official, $300 million, not counting oil aid"[29] ? Proof of MBZ's influence on Al Buhrane: the dithering over El Bechir's extradition request to The Hague to stand trial has been going on for months. In exchange for its support, the UAE probably demanded protection for its former ally by offering a local trial.

Subsequently, other cases have arisen. At the end of January 2020, several demonstrations took place in front of the UAE embassy in Khartoum, Sudan, to protest against the interference of this country in their affairs in the name of special interests, especially through human trafficking. Indeed, the Sudanese are protesting against the sending of thousands of their children to new war zones essential for the Emirates. *Nihil novi sub sole*, alas: in the summer of 2019, the Emirates leaks revealed the use of young mercenaries from Africa and transiting through Sudan, on behalf of Abu Dhabi, including its company Black Shield Security, before joining Libya and Yemen.

Al Jazeera published secret documents and information revealing the UAE's use of Sudanese airspace to transport hundreds of mercenaries that Mohammed Hamdan Diklo, Hamidati, vice president of the Sudanese Military Council, recruited from Arab tribes in Darfur and some African countries, to Libya and Yemen *via* Eritrea. A document issued by the UAE embassy to the Sudanese

---

29. https://www.jeuneafrique.com/764045/politique/au-soudan-larabie-saoudite-et-les-emirats-arabes-unis-conservent-leur-influence/

foreign affairs authorities revealed that Abu Dhabi had applied for a diplomatic permit to allow two C130 and G17 aircraft belonging to the UAE armed forces to cross and land at El Geneina airport in western Sudan. [30]

We must be moved by this lurch, otherwise we will accept the normality of conventional wars, not validated or framed by international law, which henceforth call upon untrained, unprofessional individuals who have been transformed into weapons of war without ethics or restraint. How can we describe the use of uprooted young people who have nothing left to lose, if not as the officialization of cannon fodder thanks to state mercenaries? Let us say it forcefully: the young Sudanese embarked in these endless conflicts are paying the price of their country's submission to the demands of a Gulf state trying to extend its zone of influence over the entire Arab-Muslim world. In other words, what the United Arab Emirates has put in place could be considered a war crime. It has already been established that Abu Dhabi is creating corridors for the movement of military personnel and equipment that defy all international rules of multilateralism[31].

And not only in Sudan! The Libyan conflict also requires the sending of forces to fight alongside Haftar. Both wars require a

---

30. https://www.atlantico.fr/decryptage/3586700/la-privatisation-de-la-guerre-par-les-eau-en-libye-et-au-yemen-ou-comment-abu-dhabi-re-crute-de-jeunes-soudanais-pour--leurs--guerres-sebastien-boussois
31. https://www.lemonde.fr/blog/filiu/2020/04/19/les-guerres-perdues-des-emirats-arabes-unis/

10. From Sudan to Berbera

lot of fighters. Abu Dhabi does not have the manpower. It delegates. Hence the presence of young Sudanese in the service of the Libyan National Army, signalling MBZ's ability to move its pawns forward as soon as it senses a structural vulnerability somewhere.

So it is with Ethiopia, whose conflict with Eritrea lasted 20 years. In late 2018, negotiations led to what some have called an "imported peace." This region of the Horn of Africa is critical to the stability of the Gulf. So the United Arab Emirates and Qatar were vying for the Addis Ababa regime's favor. MBZ has a head start because it dreams of setting up a base in Djibouti after extinguishing the conflict. In the meantime, the Emirati base in Assab, Eritrea, is a guarantee for MBZ to control the entry to the Gulf waters in general and the Strait of Hormuz in particular from the Indian Ocean. Above all, the base is also used in the war in Yemen.

While Qatar was still playing a mediating role until 2018, the UAE seems to have been more supportive of the ruling power by saving it economically, says one researcher.

> Ethiopia has been in the grip of social unrest for more than three years. The new reformist prime minister wants to open up the country and reposition it regionally. With this in mind, the state of emergency has been lifted, opponents have been released and reforms to liberalize the regime have been launched. Despite one of the strongest economic growth rates on the continent, the country is undergoing a major currency

crisis. The stability of its currency was only just secured by a $3 billion payment from the United Arab Emirates. Economic factors were therefore decisive in the need to conclude the peace with Eritrea.

With billions, MBZ seduces the internal power; in the name of the "war against terrorism", it seduces the external actors; by helping the Eritrean government to hold its people, it seduces the diehards.

This arm wrestling was done with American support in the context of a "global war on terrorism". However, the Eritrean regime's obstinacy seems to have paid off and this may now allow it to justify, *a posteriori*, its radical attitude towards its population. Externally, Eritrea has made military concessions to the Gulf states in the context of their war in Yemen (notably by distancing itself from Tehran). This broke its economic and diplomatic isolation and it was therefore inevitable for the regime to agree to negotiate with Ethiopia. (...) The Ethiopian and Eritrean governments did not decide alone on the direction their relationship should take. Each leader met with Emirati officials on several occasions before, during and after the reconciliation process.[32]

32. https://www.lemonde.fr/afrique/article/2018/09/28/ethiopie-eryth-ree-la-proclamation-inattendue-d-une-paix-importee_5361402_3212.html

In exchange, each pledges allegiance to the U.S. and offers privileged access to natural resources. As such, Ethiopia has two assets: water and labor. In July 2019, Ethiopian Prime Minister Abiy Ahmed announced the dispatch of 50,000 workers, officially to reduce the country's unemployment and train its workforce, but mostly to provide MBZ with cheap, malleable, unchallenging employees who are essential to future Emirati projects, starting with the Dubai 2020 World Expo. There is even talk of 200,000 workers in all! *Jackpot* for MBZ and glory for Abiy Ahmed, winner of the Nobel Peace Prize for having led his country to an agreement.

Somalia did not resist MBZ either; DP World, the Emirates' flagship port management company, was awarded the management of the port of Berbera, the only deepwater port in the Horn of Africa. Even political high-flyers know how to fish in deep waters!

11. From rebellions to reconciliations (and back)

Anwar Gargash, the UAE's Minister of State for Foreign Affairs, has stated that his country will always support Morocco. Yet Rabat rebels on occasion. Thus, as early as June 5, 2017, the kingdom spoke out against the blockade of Qatar. Intolerable, for MBZ. In June 2018, Abu Dhabi shows its wrath by voting against Morocco to host the 2026 World Cup. In March 2019, Rabat leaves the coalition involved in Yemen and led by Saudi Arabia and the UAE. Nasser Burrita, Moroccan Foreign Minister, took the opportunity to recall the sovereignty of his country, despite the "depth" of historical relations with the Gulf countries, "especially Saudi Arabia and the United Arab Emirates"[33]. The dispute dates back to more than a month ago when the minister defied Abu Dhabi by giving an interview

33. http://www.mapexpress.ma/actualite/activite-gouvernementale/nasser-bourita-la-politique-etrangere-est-une-affaire-de-souverainete-pour-le-maroc-et-la-coordination-avec-les-pays-du-golfe-doit-se-faire-de-part-et-dautre/

to Al Jazeera, the Qatari channel, while UAE nationals were banned from airing since the blockade.

In reality, tensions with Morocco are peppered with milder phases. In May 2018, Rabat broke off relations with Tehran, less to please the Emirates than to sanction Iran's indirect support for the turbulent Polisario Front. In September 2018, Mohamed VI's visit to Abu Dhabi, after several months of friction and silence. And, patatras! In December 2018, as Prince Mohamed bin Salmane began a tour of the Maghreb, it seems that Rabat has refused to welcome him. The umpteenth affront.

This desire for independence has its limits, and these limits are economic. Morocco is in dire need of Abu Dhabi's financial support. Sometimes in the form of grants: in 2013, MBZ helped create the National Initiative for Human Development (INDH) by transferring $100 million to the kingdom. But this direct support should not mask a mutual interest! According to the Moroccan Foreign Exchange Office, the UAE is Morocco's second largest trading partner in the Gulf, the first being Saudi Arabia. For its part, Abu Dhabi takes advantage of Morocco's strategic location at the crossroads of Europe, the Arab world, Africa and the Atlantic, to invest in telecoms, transport, energy and real estate. The port of Casablanca and Mohammedia were partly financed by the UAE[34].

For some years now, Emirati *soft power has been achieved* through large-scale interventions as well as through small

______

34. https://www.usinenouvelle.com/article/les-pays-du-golfe-de-modestes-partenaires-commerciaux-pour-le-maroc-mais-de-bons-pour-voyeurs-de-capitaux.N292140

micro-economic initiatives. Let's focus on one example. In 2019, the country's ambassador came to the aid of the local populations of Beni Mellal affected by cold waves.

In a speech delivered at a ceremony attended by the wali of the region of Beni Mellal-Khenifra, governor of the province of Beni Mellal, Abdeslam Bekrate and associations and institutions of social welfare beneficiaries, the Emirati diplomat said that this humanitarian operation is part of the very strong friendly relations between the two sister countries. It aims to mitigate the effects of the cold wave in favor of mountain populations, adding that it is organized in accordance with the guidelines of Sheikh Khalifa bin Zayed Al Nahyane, President of the United Arab Emirates.

This aid is also supported and monitored by the Crown Prince of Abu Dhabi, Deputy Supreme Commander of the Armed Forces of the United Arab Emirates, Sheikh Mohammed bin Zayed Al Nahyane. He also said that this aid, which includes winter quilts and foodstuffs, is also part of several other operations covering the entire national territory, which is able to further strengthen the cooperation and solidarity between Morocco and the United Arab Emirates.[35]

---

35. https://www.leseco.ma/maroc/73484-beni-mellal-khenifra-don-des-Émirats united-arabes-populations-facing-winter-cold.html

11. From rebellions to reconciliations (and back)

How difficult it seems to resist the Emirati call and its fortune! Even those who try for a moment to resist politically find themselves under his control thanks to his fatal weapon: the sovereign wealth fund. Simultaneously, MBZ continued its undermining work against the Islamists of the PJD, in government since 2012, which displeases the UAE president. In January 2019, former Prime Minister Abdellilah Benkirane accused UAE of relentless harassment[36]. In short, between seduction operations and attempts to interfere on the one hand, well understood financial interest and sporadic rebellion on the other, the relationship between the two countries fluctuates.

At the end of 2019, the Trump administration revived bilateral relations between the two partners[37]. Once again, sport is a symbol: Morocco and the United Arab Emirates agree to take part in the Arab Gulf Cup, which will be held in Qatar on November 26. For its part, the United States was pleased that a new common front against Iran was emerging. In exchange, at the end of 2019, Trump came in person to sign a defense contract of one billion dollars with Morocco. *Business is business!*

---

36. https://www.yabiladi.com/articles/details/73645/abdelilah-ben-kirane-accuse-emirats-arabes.html
37. https://www.middleeasteye.net/fr/decryptages/un-accord-politique-entre-trump-et-mohammed-vi-serait-derriere-le-rapprochement-maroc

12. From war to *business*

After nine years of war, Bashar al-Assad's continued rule
and the defeat of Daech are bringing Syria back under stable
authoritarianism. MBZ sees juicy prospects. As of January 8,
2019, Emirati and Bahraini embassies reopen in Damascus
while most Westerners drag their feet[38]. The official objective:
to counter Iranian influence - the attentive reader knows that
it is either that or the fight against terrorism! Nevertheless, by
positioning itself in this way, MBZ once again defies the reso-
lutions and sanctions of the United Nations that condemn
Syria, and sides with Moscow. On March 15, 2019, is signed
an agreement between Russia and the United Arab Emirates,
which allows the Emirates to become the first economic
partner of Syria[39].

---

38. https://www.aljazeera.com/indepth/opinion/uae-bahrain-open-em-
bassies-syria-190107165601089.html
39. https://agsiw.org/uae-and-russia-find-common-ground-on-syria/

However, in 2011, the UAE was supporting rebel groups against Bashar al-Assad's regime while maintaining some relations with Damascus. The war in Yemen led the UAE to withdraw from the Syrian field. Nevertheless, Emirati businessmen remained on the lookout...

> By the end of 2011, the UAE had begun to welcome Syrian businessmen residing in the UAE and opposed to the Damascus regime. In November 2012, the Dubai Chamber of Commerce and Industry organized a conference titled "A Partnership to Invest in Syria's Future" under the patronage of the UAE Ministry of Foreign Affairs and with the participation of many UAE-based Syrian businessmen to boost the economy in the post-Assad era. The Syrian businessmen present at the conference said they would invest 1 billion US dollars in various sectors of the Syrian economy (real estate, services, health and education) in case of the fall of the Assad regime[40].

As quickly as possible, Emirati delegations are rushing to Syria, because reconstruction is urgent. By contributing, along with Russia, to the resurrection of this ravaged country, the UAE is supporting the dictator who has caused the death of hundreds of thousands of Syrians. Faced with the general opprobrium, the entrepreneurs must therefore remain discreet. In the Syrian capital, the Emirati flag is no

---

40. https://cadmus.eui.eu/handle/1814/64727

United Arab Emirates conquering the world

longer hidden, but the 38 businessmen present at the 2019 Damascus International Fair avoided the media. The U.S. Embassy had been clear: "It is unacceptable and inappropriate for businessmen, individuals and chambers of commerce outside Syria to participate."[41] According to Washington, Abu Dhabi should therefore be subject to international sanctions. Pass the nutmeg! In reality, the UAE is gradually increasing its engagement with Syria in the form of humanitarian aid and investment in the entertainment sector. During the last weeks of Ramadan 2019, food parcels are being distributed in Marjeh Square in central Damascus, with the UAE emblem. The truck carrying the aid carried a sign that read, "Gift from Her Highness Sheikha Latifa Bin Mohammad Ben Rashid al-Maktoum, wife of the Crown Prince of Al Fujairah, one of the seven emirates of the United Arab Emirates." [42]

In Syria, MBZ does not have one priority, it has three:
- real estate,
- transportation and
- trade.

Emirati businessmen do not seem to be sulking. In December 2018, Damac Properties, one of the largest real estate developers in the UAE and the Arab world, sent a delegation to Damascus to meet with representatives of two Syrian companies, Telsa Group and al-Diyar al-Dimashqiah.

---

41. https://www.middleeasteye.net/news/uae-business-delegation-syria-turns-heads-and-avoids-media-attention
42. https://www.asiatimes.com/2019/05/article/uae-using-soft-power-in-syria-after-7-year-frost/

The owner of the latter is Mohammad Ghazi al-Jalali, a former minister of communications and minority shareholder who sits on the board of Syriatel. More generally, UAE real estate development companies such as Reportage Properties, Rotana, Arabtec and Horizon Energy LLC were well represented at the 2019 Damascus International Fair. On the tourism side, it also got off to an early start, as evidenced by the approval of a four-star hotel restoration that fell in July 2018 to UAE's Coral Hotels and its local partner Julia Dumna for approximately US$1.7 million.

On the transportation side, the UAE does not intend to be outdone. In 2017, it was the seventh or eighth largest market for Syrian exporters, accounting for US$44.5 million, mostly through

- fats and oils ;
- articles made of stone, asbestos and similar materials;
- pearls, precious and semi-precious stones and metals; and
- coffee, tea, mate and spices.

However, the balance of trade was clearly in the UAE's favor, with exports to Syria approaching US$1 billion in the same year, and increasing by 50% the following year... even if this figure is a deception allowed by the mass of Chinese products transiting through Dubai to be relabelled "Emirati". DP World is on the alert, as Syria is a unique gateway to the Mediterranean Sea. In early January 2019, the company announced the creation of a 2,500 km transport corridor linking Jebel Ali (Dubai)

United Arab Emirates conquering the world

to the Nassib-Jaber border crossing between Jordan and Syria. The terminal operator said the new corridor would enable close collaboration between customs authorities and logistics service providers from the UAE, Saudi Arabia, Jordan, Syria and Lebanon to create a more efficient flow of goods to and from Syria. The time savings are considerable, with transport officially reduced from 24 to 6 days.

The ties between the UAE and Syria are strong, important and in part reciprocal. Indeed, the Syrian community has always been very present in the UAE. Traditionally inclined towards *business*, Syrian emigrants have played, since 2011, an essential intermediary role in order not to lose sight of the contractual prospects that would open up after the end of the conflict. Since the Syrian revolution, the UAE has extended residence permits to more than 100,000 Syrians, including 6,000 investors, academics, entrepreneurs. By the end of 2020, 240,000 Syrians were living in the UAE, mainly in construction, media, health and tourism.

13. From Marib to Djibouti

For many heads of state, *business* and geopolitical influence will always take precedence over ethical considerations. This is illustrated by the activities of MBZ in Chechnya, where Vladimir Putin has imposed the rule of Ramzan Kadyrov since 2007. The objective is now well known: to serve as a safeguard against the resurgence of radical Islam, which Putin had overcome by razing Grozny in 2000. Regularly, Kadyrov is invited with great pomp and warmth by MBZ in the Emirates. All occasions are good: Ramadan, tourism, vacations, sports events. Good accounts make good friends, and the UAE invests a lot in the country, its official objective being in line with that of Russia.

In 2016, Abu Dhabi organized a major Islamic conference to emphasize the fundamentals of Sunni orthodoxy. Yet Kadyrov peppers his speeches with haunting "Allah Akbar," a sign that he is a champion of an Islam that is, at the very least, strict and tolerated by his Russian neighbor and sponsor. Neither

Putin nor MBZ are offended by his remarks about women and homosexuals, nor do they call on him to moderate his outbursts against other countries. The preservation of an ally in the North Caucasus region is also at this price[43] !

It is this same pragmatism that guides the UAE's behaviour in Yemen. The region is loaded with significance for both the UAE and Saudi Arabia: the Al Nahyan tribe, which has spread to the north of the peninsula, originated there. Yemen is thus perceived as the cradle of origins. This is another reason why the Emirates have set out to reinvest in it and make it a solid state. Obviously, the ethnological justification is backed by a *business* project, as summarized to me at the end of October 2019 the researcher Bassam Taham, during an interview.

For some years now, the Emirates have been aware that they would soon run out of oil. So they thought of Yemen. In history, the ports of Yemen, the best known of which are Aden and Hodeida, are very important places, once exploited by the Portuguese and then by the British. The war in which the UAE got involved as early as 2015 allowed them to pursue their dream of investing there. Miscalculation: the Iranians had no intention of giving up the place to them. So they supported the Houthis.

Yemen is a country of political failures. The failure of the rebels who believed in a Yemeni Spring in 2011; the failure

---

43. https://www.lemonde.fr/blog/filiu/2020/12/13/les-liaisons-dangere-uses-des-emirats-avec-des-ennemis-declares-de-la-france/

United Arab Emirates conquering the world

of Saudi Arabia, the UAE and France, who supported the repression of the rebellion. In this sense, the determination of Riyadh and Abu Dhabi to take control of the country at all costs, no matter how many people die, is significant. In addition to the geostrategy of controlling the sea lanes, there is the project of establishing a political and ideological annex. In the eyes of MBZ, there is no question of the Shiite revolution gangrening the boot of the peninsula, nor of Iran taking the two countries in a vice-like grip by supporting with impunity the Houthi rebellion that is rampant in the South. The head of state is wary of both Tehran and Sayed Hasan, spokesman for the Yemeni armed forces. Hasn't Hasan said that, as soon as he wished, he would be able to pull down the glass towers of the arrogant, capitalist, Western-compromised Dubai[44] ? This threat must be dealt with as soon as possible.

All the more so since establishing its domination over Yemen means gaining ground in the Arab world. Indeed, the princely family comes from the Al Bu Falah tribe, a branch of the Bani Yas tribal confederation, whose ancestors would take root in the region of Marib. Marib is the region of origin of many Arab tribes, in this case the Qahtanids, the Arabs of the South. Moreover, the city is home to a founding monument: a dam reputed to have been built three millennia earlier. Now in ruins, it was one of the marvels of ancient engineering; and it still constitutes the keystone of the diaspora of the local tribes.

---

44. https://lecridespeuples.fr/2019/09/23/le-yemen-menace-de-faire-vol-er-en-eclats-les-tours-de-verre-de-dubai-et-dabu-dhabi/

13. From Marib to Djibouti

Indeed, its collapse, around the year 575, led to the definitive failure of the irrigation system. As a result, many tribes had to leave for other regions of the Arabian Peninsula - this has been called the "ethnic Gulf Stream" of the Arab tribes.

The city of Marib has a special significance for Sheikh Zayed bin Sultan Al Nahyan, the founder of the United Arab Emirates. So much so that, in 1984, he ordered the reconstruction of the dam to provide water and electricity to the region of Sana'a and Marib. He personally financed the $100 million project and inaugurated it on December 26, 1986. MBZ has visited Marib many times. His pride in his Yemeni heritage is no secret. Sheikh Zayed even invited Yemenis from the Marib region to come to the UAE, granting them Emirati citizenship by virtue of their ancestral tribal roots. Hundreds of Socotrans have also settled in the Emirate of Ajman. Along the way, the population of Yemeni origin in the UAE has become significant. Among its nationals, there are many *traders* from Dubai... and some very rich individuals who have invested their wealth in Abu Dhabi or Dubai. Perhaps the most notable example is the family of the late President Ali Abdullah Saleh, who was said to have accumulated a fortune of between $30 and $60 billion over 33 years in power, and whose eldest son, Ahmed Ali Saleh, remains MBZ's unwelcome guest in Abu Dhabi.

In this context, which is multi-millennial and spiced with both financial and geostrategic stakes, the UAE is particularly sensitive to the turmoil in Yemen. They have been a party to the war since March 2015. On November 24, 2015,

MBZ received at Al Shati Palace the chiefs and dignitaries of the Marib tribes, led by the governor of Marib Sultan Ben Ali Al Arrada. Accompanying them was Brigadier Mussalam Al Rashedi, commander of the Marib Liberation Force, which participates in the Arab-Sunni coalition against the Houthis. Nevertheless, in this deadly quagmire, nothing is simple and everything is complicated. MBZ's motivation seems clear: it is to contain Iran by containing the restless Houthis on the southern borders of the Saudi kingdom. The reality is more complicated.

For example, Abu Dhabi decided to support the secessionist aspirations of the Southern Transitional Council, even though they are theoretically allies of President Abd Rabbo Mansour Hadi. Another example: the United Arab Emirates expressed in July 2019 its willingness to disengage operationally in Yemen. Except that, in reality, this real-fake withdrawal does not change anything, insofar as Abu Dhabi retains local militia relays trained and well established, responsible for preserving its immediate interests - in this case, the control of the coast-lines of the southern Arabian Peninsula in order to ensure the control of maritime communication routes and straits.

Learning from their territorial dispute over the islands of Abu Musa and Lesser and Greater Tomb, the United Arab Emirates have developed a strategy to secure their shipping lanes[45] that pass through the Straits of Hormuz and Bab el

---

45. https://www.lemonde.fr/international/article/2018/06/01/les-Émirats united-arabes-architects-of-a-new-maritime-empire_5308119_3210.html

Mandeb. *Ceteris paribus*, it is the Chinese strategy known as the "string of pearls": to ensure that the routes remain open to its ships, it is necessary to build ports and military bases along the maritime spaces to be controlled. Hence the presence of the UAE in the Horn of Africa, the Arabian Sea, the Red Sea and even in the Indian Ocean, in the Maldives, the Seychelles and the Comoros. Thanks to the oil and gas windfall, boosted by the takeover of Socotra Island, Abu Dhabi is actively financing a policy of influence on the African coast, with varying degrees of success. The deal is successful in Eritrea thanks to the signing of a lease on the port of Assab in 2015; it remains uncertain in Somaliland; and it failed in Djibouti, after the cancellation of agreements in February 2018. Surprising but reassuring: even the power of MBZ sometimes meets insurmountable resistance...

14. From crime to failure

Its symbolic and geostrategic motives should not hide the reality of the war in Yemen. It is one of the most serious humanitarian crises of recent years. Between 2015 and 2019, it has killed more than 100,000 victims, including at least 80,000 children. However, these terrible figures only reveal part of the disaster. We must also mention the two million displaced Yemenis, the famine, poverty and lack of drinking water caused by the bombardments that have lasted four years and resulted in almost zero for the coalition. By 2021, 70% of the population no longer has access to clean water; 50% has no access to health care; and 80% of Yemenis are dependent on humanitarian aid.

According to the International Committee of the Red Cross, in the first six months of 2019 alone, more than 3 million people have benefited from the organization's water activities; nearly 400,000 people have received various forms of assistance including food, 7,000 detainees have been provided access to clean water, and 255,000 patients have received emergency care. For Human Rights Watch, there is evidence that since 2015, at least 90 international coalition strikes have deliberately targeted civilians, homes, schools, hospitals, mosques, weddings, or buses filled with children[46].

The Emirati-Saudi tandem is also accused of having used chemical weapons. Jamal Khashoggi was allegedly murdered because he was about to reveal such facts, which would have forced the international community to react despite its complacency for MBZ[47]. Infringement of the 1997 chemical weapons ban, signed and ratified by Saudi Arabia, war crimes and crimes against humanity would no longer have allowed the silence of nations to continue. This would have been double justice: for the victims and against Saudi Arabia, which in April 2018, through the Arab League, was still demanding an investigation into the chemical weapons allegedly used by the Damascus regime. According to a person close to the journalist, the state assassins acted against Jamal Khashoogi while Britain was aware of the conspiracy going on. The accusation needs to be substantiated, but it is not absurd. Britain and the United States support the anti-Houthi intervention. If the UAE and Saudi Arabia fell, would they not have been splashed as well?

Among the warfare techniques that may be of concern, the activities of the company Black Shield, which we mentioned

___

46. https://www.hrw.org/fr/world-report/2019/country-chapters/326295
47. https://www.express.co.uk/news/world/1037378/Khashoggi-mur-der-news-saudi-arabia-chemical-weapons-use

earlier, are not the least shocking. The company recruits young people from Sudan, Chad and Uganda as cannon fodder under the pretext of training them in the UAE to guard the UAE borders. As soon as they arrive, their papers and phones are confiscated before they are taken to the front. None of them returned.

It was after seeing the controversy rise that MBZ decided to announce its withdrawal from Yemen. The credibility of this statement may be questionable. Why have hoped for so long for a favorable outcome for him when the experts gave, from the outset, the coalition losing with the entry of Iran in support of the Houthis? In April 2019, Saudi Arabia and the UAE were still congratulating themselves on Donald Trump's strategic choice not to have voted for a resolution demanding an end to the bombing, the coalition's intervention and the massacres. So, how can we explain, three months later, the pusillanimous versatility that seems to be reflected in the reversal? In addition to media pressure, the desire not to increase tensions with Iran may have played a role. After all, failing to install a government at its beck and call, the Emirates and Saudi Arabia had succeeded in part in their bid to contain Tehran.

Today, the clear failure of the UAE and its affiliate (who wanted to stay in Yemen), despite the massacres and torture inflicted on the Yemenis, proves that only a negotiated solution to the crisis is possible. However, the political solution is dragging on so long that there is a great risk of seeing the

14. From crime to failure

emergence of military powers, encouraged by the complicit indifference of the international community. Not to act diplomatically would be more than a grave error: it would be another crime added to all those that are already known and documented.

However, it is a safe bet that counting on Paris to sound the charge would be utopian. There are at least three reasons why France would be more than a little embarrassed to challenge the Emirates on this issue.

First, the UAE is considered by Emmanuel Macron's team to be "the only real trusted partner" among the petro-monarchies: this is what the Élysée stipulated on the occasion of Mohammed ben Zayed Al Nahyan's visit to Paris on November 8, 2017. The proximity between the two states is a differentiating marker of his policy, into which the French president nevertheless tries to inject a dose of his famous "at the same time." As Olivier Da Lage summarized it to me, during an interview,

> Nicolas Sarkozy relied on Qatar, François Hollande on Saudi Arabia; Emmanuel Macron has marked his difference by strengthening ties with the Emirates without breaking with either Qatar or Saudi Arabia. It is all a matter of degree. With the UAE, the military dimension is essential, insofar as the French base in Abu Dhabi is the only one France has in the Middle East, and military cooperation between France and the

Emirates is both long-standing and very close (as it is with Qatar, for that matter).

Olivier Da Lage puts his finger on the problem: the second reason that would restrain France, assuming it had the desire to confront the UAE with the reality of its abuses, lies in the military dimension of this "partnership of trust. On the one hand, the geographical position of the UAE is essential for the French army; on the other hand, between January 2008 and July 2017, the UAE ranked sixth in French arms exports. If we add exports to Saudi Arabia, which ranks second, we come close to 15 billion euros in sales[48]. The report to Parliament on French arms exports in 2021 qualified the statement over one year: the United States was now only the ninth largest importer, but Saudi Arabia had snatched first place from the United States, so that, in total, the two friends accounted for 833.3 million euros in 2020, i.e., 16 per cent of a market that was in sharp decline due, officially, to the health crisis[49]. It would be highly inappropriate to upset such good clients, who alone represent 1/6 of French arms exports!

A third reason, linking the UAE and France in a quasi Faustian pact, literature aside, synthesizes the first two: French-made CAESAR guns have been used in the Yemeni conflict. Positioned on the Saudi border, they are officially

---

48. https://www.vie-publique.fr/sites/default/files/rapport/pdf/184000683.pdf
49. https://www.lemonde.fr/international/article/2021/06/03/paris-met-l-accent-sur-ses-ventes-d-armes-a-l-europe_6082652_3210.html

14. From crime to failure

used for defensive purposes but, with their 42-kilometer range, they also "support loyalist troops, backed up by Saudi armed forces, in their advance into Yemeni territory. Let us specify that the author of this revelation is not an investigator from a local NGO that a suspicious mind would sweep aside with a wave of the hand or a contemptuous frown. It is an authentic note from the Directorate of Military Intelligence (DRM), revealed by *Disclose* and Arte[50]. The official body estimates that 437,000 people may be affected by bombings. However, according to the investigative site, 52 artillery shots were fired at the perimeters exclusively covered by these French guns, killing 35 civilians.

And that's not all! It is attested that Leclerc tanks, sold by France to the United Arab Emirates, are used during coalition offensives on Yemeni territory, according to *Disclose* journalists. Worse, if "worse" still has any meaning in the light of these infamies, French weapons are being used to starve the already starving population. Among others, several French-made helicopters are participating in the blockade of the port of Al-Hodeïda[51], serving a "starvation strategy"[52], which is also supported by a frigate modernized by Naval Group, a French

---

50. https://made-in-france.disclose.ngo/fr/chapter/yemen-papers/ and https://www.arte.tv/fr/videos/086089-022-A/yemen-des-armes-made-in-france/
51. "A "confidential-defense" note details the use of French weapons in Yemen," *Le Monde*, April 15, 2019
52. "Revelations: here is the map of French weapons in Yemen, according to a confidential defense report," *France Inter*, April 15, 2019

company[53], and other French helicopters rushed to the heart of the maritime blockade organized by the coalition[54].

These revelations constitute a state lie uttered on France Inter by Florence Parly, then Minister of the Armed Forces, in January 2019, when she claimed "to have no proof that French weapons were the cause of civilian casualties in Yemen." The much earlier DRM report proves the contrary. The minister knew, without the slightest doubt, that "contrary to the official discourse in Paris, the equipment sold to Riyadh is used offensively and not simply defensively"[55], which is prohibited by the conventions to which France is a signatory. The involvement of tricolored weapons in Yemen is a glaring example of troubled links between the Emirati sphere and the Hexagon; but it is not the only one, far from it!

53. *France Culture*, August 16, 2018. See also Anne Poiret, *Mon pays vend des armes*, Les Arènes, May 2019
54. "Blockade of Yemen: videos prove the participation of ships sold by France", *Mediapart,*September 17, 2019
55. "French weapons in Yemen: the missile document", *Liberation,* 15 April 2019.

15. From the battle of the train to the conquest of the mosques

In recent years, the relationship between France and the UAE has not only been commercial in general and military in particular. It is also, notably,

- political (in order to play a role in managing the upheavals in the Middle East, France must maintain strong ties with the Gulf countries) and
- religious (the UAE and Saudi Arabia expect to influence political Islam in France).

In all these respects, even if the link has sometimes been weakened, Paris is historically close to the Gulf countries. Jacques Chirac was a great friend of King Abdullah. Even Nicolas Sarkozy, though reputedly pro-American and pro-Israeli, was able to establish a relationship of trust with the said Abdullah... before his closeness to Bashar al-Assad, displayed on the Champs-Élysées during the July 14, 2008 parade, infuriated the Saudi monarch. France's failure in the tender for the high-speed line linking Mecca to Medina (the Spanish won) did not help to dissipate the anger. Today, some persist in accusing Nicolas Sarkozy of having sold his country to Qatar, an emirate capable of

- to invest in the world to ensure its future when oil runs out, and
- to distribute the dream by buying the Paris-Saint-Germain soccer club.

From 2012, François Hollande shows his willingness to reach an agreement with Iran. Laurent Fabius, his Minister of Foreign Affairs, committed himself to this without hesitation. These provisions reassure Saudi Arabia and contribute to rebuild the link between France and the UAE. In 2017, Emmanuel Macron took over the Élysée Palace and tried to balance the two sides. Thus, a few months after his election, he inaugurated the Louvre in Abu Dhabi and then went to Riyadh and Doha, just to show his attachment to the three Gulf countries.

Abu Dhabi is particularly fond of the French president's political tone. The law on separatism and the new promotion of a "French-style secularism" give him two opportunities to rub his hands. Indeed, the UAE joins Paris on two lines: the fight against terrorism (in France, against radical Islam); and secularism (which echoes, in the UAE, the brakes on the Muslim Brotherhood). The two lines are linked. Based on the idea of a struggle against an armed danger, they illustrate what Andreas Krieg has called the *weaponization of* narratives[56].

---

56. https://www.researchgate.net/publication/331436035_The_Weapon-ization_of_Narratives_Amid_the_Gulf_Crisis_The_Anatomy_of_a_Crisis

However, beyond the diplomatic exchanges under the spotlight, it is also in the religious field that the relationship between the Emirates, Saudi Arabia and France is played out. This is evidenced by the battle over French mosques. Basically, these are mainly controlled by three states:

- Turkey,

- Morocco and

- Algeria.

Nevertheless, the distribution is neither as clear nor as stable as it seems. Thus, despite its appetite as devouring as that of its competitors, Turkey, pointed out by an Italian senator for financing half of the French mosques, only controls one sixth of the 2,600 Muslim places of worship in France. Of course, it provides 50% of the seconded imams, officially sent by the Turkish government to make up for the lack of French imams; but they represent less than a tenth of the imams installed in France (between 1,500 and 1,800). Moreover, Turkish Islam is itself divided between the moderate branch of the Ditlib, under the control of the Turkish Ministry of Religious Affairs, and the Millî Görüş Islamic Confederation, which is close to the Muslim Brotherhood and recently came under the spotlight on the occasion of the proposed municipal subsidy outline to support the Strasbourg mosque project[57].

Therefore, it is complex, to say the least, to formally evaluate the distribution of foreign influences on French Islam. The

---

57. https://www.lemonde.fr/les-decodeurs/article/2020/11/05/que-pese-vraiment-la-turquie-dans-l-islam-de-france_6058644_4355770.html

15. From the battle of the train to the conquest of the mosques

opacity of sometimes contradictory figures thickens the debate. The volatility of the situation sharpens the appetites of the various factions involved. It is in this context that the Gulf States are more and more openly assuming their ambition to become an important player. For a long time in the background, they were traditionally considered to be close to Turkey. But, curiously, despite the means available to the Emiratis, Abu Dhabi's attempts to enter the game do not always seem to succeed.

Thus, in 2019, a former Emirati minister attended an *iftar* (a meal taken after sunset during Ramadan) in the mosque of Evry-Courcouronnes. Surprising, because the mosque of Evry is governed by the Union of Mosques of France, close to Morocco. The pressure of the kingdom has quickly meant to the Emirati dignitary, in case he had come on location, that this place of worship was a guarded hunt. The warning must have seemed credible enough to push Abu Dhabi to change its target and to think even bigger.

Direction, this time, the *nec plus ultra* of the French mosque: the Great Mosque of Paris, founded in 1926 by the Moroccan sultan Moulay Youssef.

The affair takes place on May 5, 2020. The media are then more focused on the health crisis than on Ramadan. So it was on that day that Chems-Eddine Hafiz, a lawyer of Algerian origin, elected rector of the Grand Mosque of Paris and vice-president of the French Council of the Muslim Faith, denounced the fact that the executive allowed the organization of religious gatherings for Christians on Pentecost, at the end of the month, and not for the feast of Eid. This expression of anger might seem spontaneous. Wrong: it is heavily loaded with symbolism.

First, it expresses an internal tension that continues to grow within the first mosque of France, between secular moderates, on the one hand, and, on the other hand, radicals sensitive to foreign influences ever more pressing. In other words, the struggle is in full swing between peaceful Moroccans and fiery Algerians. And Chems-Eddine Hafiz has the following ideas: on May 19, 2021, he concludes a partnership between the Great Mosque and the Licra to encourage "educational actions (...) and a common production of analyses concerning for example anti-Muslim racism, secularism, universalism and republican values. In doing so, the imam continues to expand his web by structuring the "pole of Muslim federations resulting from the fracturing of the French Council of the Muslim Faith"[58].

What is the place of the Emirates in this plate tectonics that is shaking the practice of Islam in France? For the moment, it seems to be linked to Algerian actors. Indeed, the UAE has invested a lot in an Algeria that has long been in bad shape. In 2021, their political influence on Algiers is no longer an open secret. Also, behind the criticism of the asymmetrical secularism that France would practice, one suspects the murky game of the UAE *via* its new Algerian friends.

---

58. https://www.lemonde.fr/societe/article/2021/05/20/contre-le-racisme-antimusulman-la-licra-et-la-grande-mosquee-s-allient_6080787_3224.html

According to this conjecture, Chems-Eddine Hafiz's attack would seek to assert his own line as much as to give pledges to the Emiratis and, more broadly, to all of Africa. In May 2021, did he not say that his initiative was supported by the French Federation of Islamic Associations of Africa, the Comoros and the Antilles? Nothing illogical: partly thanks to the Emirati support, Algeria is regaining a place of choice in the continent. This rise in power is reinforced by the retreat of France, whose presence and action are increasingly contested. From then on, denouncing France's Islamophobia allows the Hexagon to be chafed on its own soil, after having driven it out of Africa.

A detail confirms this hypothesis: on a poster circulating on the internet, an engraving illustrating the Great Mosque of Paris illustrates a call for respect of the confinement. However, in the upper left corner, the logo of the World Council of Muslim Communities appears. Chaired by Ali Rashid Al Nuaimi, this council, of Emirati origin and reputedly close to the intelligence services of Abu Dhabi, is behind the religious offensives underway in Europe.

What can we conclude from these elements, macroscopic or microscopic? Perhaps that a new foreign power should not be allowed to infiltrate French Islam, while the Emiratis and the Saudis have understood that their money and their connections give them a voice that can carry weight - and not only in France! Thus, in 2020, the struggle for power within the Executive of the Muslims of Belgium saw the victory of the Belgian-Moroccan Salah Echalaoui. He hopes to contain the historical influence of Wahhabi and Salafist Islam in Saudi Arabia. Even if the problematic, the specific nomenclatures and the stakes may seem complex to the uninitiated, it is advisable to be careful about the source of funds likely to support the development of a European Islam rearranged in the Abu Dhabi fashion, that is to say a radical Islam, little adapted, despite their diversity, to the specificities of Western Muslims.

16. From the dark depths to the jewels of the Emirates

In this very religious context, it may seem curious that a federation of emirates that seems to have a project to develop an Islam of its own in France should invest in a political issue by saving from disaster a party whose pro-Muslim tropism is not its main characteristic. Yet, it is one more link between the Emirates and France that Mediapart revealed, at the end of June 2017, by showing how the National Front was saved from the UAE. As incredible as it sounds, the Lepenist party was able to file balanced campaign accounts thanks to an 8 million euro loan from an Emirati bank, intermediary between the party and Noor Capital. Noor, "light" in Arabic, is an asset management company based in Abu Dhabi.

At the helm of this contract signed in the Central African Republic is Laurent Foucher, an entrepreneur in the straight line of the old Françafrique. In his defense, the man claims to have made a good deal, insofar as his loan allowed the party to be reimbursed for its campaign expenses of about six million euros, thus reimbursing him the capital and the 6% interest over eight months. As *Marianne* pointed out, this is not without irony: in 2016, an MEP "strategy and economic adviser to Marine Le Pen" had vetoed funding "from the Middle East" because, he explained, "if we accepted, we would no longer be credible"[59].

One hypothesis has been raised: in reality, Noor Capital could also be an intermediary between high Emirati dignitaries and the party, which is accustomed to sulphurous support - hadn't the lepénistes benefited a few years earlier from a Russian payment? This possibility is surprising. The Front - now, in 2018, Rassemblement - National is not known for its inclination towards Islam and its followers. Why would a Muslim country support such a political fraction?

It is unlikely that this is a case of adding fuel to the fire by encouraging islamophobic expression to exacerbate tensions. On the other hand, it is possible that the Lepéniste movement, like other European governments with governments close to a far-right ideology, is seen as a practical safeguard against the radical Islam symbolized, in the eyes of the UAE, by the Muslim Brotherhood. In this sense, supporting the Front would have been a kind of foreshadowing of support for Emmanuel Macron's secularist policy, an anti-freedom speech being worth a temporary transfer of eight million dollars...

---

59. https://www.marianne.net/politique/comptes-de-campagne-ces-8-millions-venus-des-emirats-qui-ont-sauve-le-fn-en-2017

The rescue of the National Front further weaves the not always honorable ties between the UAE and France; and the strangest thing is that one could multiply the examples of the tricks deployed by the Emirates to become official or unofficial actors in the life of France. Indeed, the arms trade, religion, and politics are just some of the elements included in their panoply. The ability to influence a partner's perception of a country is another. We need to look at two cases here: that of a lobbyist and that of a journalist.

The first case is that of the astute Elyes Ben Chedly, *businessman* and lobbyist. This Tunisian, well introduced in the Sarkozyist nebula and a great adept of shell companies, as revealed by the Panama Papers, has worked in the highest spheres of his country of origin, but also in Libya, Kazakhstan and the United Arab Emirates. A skilled intermediary, he served, for example, as a tourist guide to Patrick Balkany in Mauritania or, even more profitable, as an intermediary between EADS and Astana (in 2015, an internal audit of Airbus would have stipulated, among other things, that he had been paid nearly ten million euros for facilitating the sale of two satellites to the Kazakhs).

In the Emirates, more precisely in the emirate of Ras al Khaimah, our man founded an import-export company alongside two relatives of high dignitaries. Thanks to his links with Bassam Freiha, who knows the big names of the Arab world... and vice versa, the merchant gradually imposes himself and manages to sneak in Mohamed ben Zayed. As soon as Emmanuel Macron is elected, despite the accusations that pursue him, he gets closer to LREM through some deputies, seeming to play the role of a salesman for MBZ. Thus, on December 2, 2018, he organized a well-attended event at the Louvre to commemorate the centenary of Sheik Zayed. Since then, he would continue a lobbyist activity, evidenced for example by the former MP LREM Gregory Galbadon, vice president of the Group of Friendship France - United Arab Emirates from 2017 to 2018... before firing his cutie in favor of Qatar, which he will defend forcefully in 2019 for the 2022 soccer World Cup[60], even if it means stirring up the expected controversy[61].

One thing is clear: Qatar and the UAE are engaged in a fierce competition to win over opinion makers in the political arena, as we have just outlined, but also among the general public. Abu Dhabi, for example, can count on the enthusiasm of a strong advocate in this regard.

The second case we would like to outline is that of the great *reporter* Georges Malbrunot. The former hostage, along with Christian Chesnot, his fellow hostage, has written two virulent books against Doha. Nevertheless, in the race for opinion, not all blows are allowed! After accusing a senator of having been paid by Qatar, the two authors were convicted

---

60. https://www.lepoint.fr/sport/oui-la-coupe-du-monde-de-football-2022-peut-se-tenir-au-qatar-08-10-2019-2340088_26.php
61. https://www.marianne.net/agora/humeurs/comment-deux-deputes-lrem-peuvent-ils-defendre-un-etat-aussi-corrompu-que-le-qatar

of defamation[62]. However, even after the passage of justice, the impact of "revelations" remains, always more effective in the media than a detailed dive into the complexity of the Gulf countries. This is what it is all about: anti-Qatari criticism or pro-Emirates panegyrics aim to spread the idea that the UAE is "our only real partner" in the "fight against terrorism" but not only in this context, as Georges Malbrunot stated during a conference given in January 2020 on the occasion of a cruise entitled Jewels of the Emirates".

The phenomenon is not reserved for MBZ lobbies: the desire to influence French opinion, manifested underhandedly by several foreign countries, is worrying enough for Stéphane Bouillon, the head of the General Secretariat for Defense and National Security (SGDSN), to announce, in June 2021, the creation of a "service with national competence in charge of tracking down foreign interference in the field of information"[63]. Although their entryism is not as famous as the Russian attempts, the U.S. does not hesitate to engage in the struggle for influence.

Recently, reputable media outlets with boilerplate titles have been taken over in recent years to disseminate news and articles favorable to the UAE and Saudi Arabia in a covert manner, while being - oh surprise!- very critical of the

---

62. https://www.europe1.fr/politique/une-senatrice-fait-condamner-le-livre-nos-tres-chers-emirs-en-diffamation-3760784
63. https://www.lemonde.fr/international/article/2021/06/03/le-gouvernement-va-creer-un-service-charge-de-lutter-contre-les-ingerences-etrangeres-dans-les-medias_6082708_3210.html

Qatari neighbor. This is the case of *La Lettre A, Intelligence online* and *Africa online. La Lettre A,* a "daily newspaper of influence and power", proposes to "unveil the strategies of influence that impact political decisions, anticipates the changes in large companies and deciphers the transformations of media power". 40 years old, *La Lettre A* presents itself on its website as one of the titles of the Indigo group, "an independent press company".

This "independent" group is worth looking into. It has an annual turnover of 3 million euros, which rose by 1.2 million euros in September 2019. A private study reveals that the majority of the 1200 new online connections on *Intelligence online* were based in Saudi Arabia, which was not the case at all before February 2019. The number one target is France. A budget of one million euros per year is dedicated to the Hexagon. The other new connections come partly from French-speaking countries such as Morocco, Niger, Mauritania or Vietnam. For *Africa online,* in 2018, there were about 900 connections from the UAE and none from Saudi Arabia. Between February 2019 and September 2019, the connections have increased to 1700 from the UAE and 1600 from Saudi Arabia. The same study shows that the bulk of connections to Indigo Group sites in 2018 and 2019 came from France at 60%. There is no financial revenue from advertising on these three sites. Subscriptions to the group's publications and the purchase of specific articles range between 300 and 1000 euros, which proves that the target audience is primarily professional. As for the *Lettre A,* the same process: few visits coming from the Gulf countries before February 2019, then explosion of connections coming from Riyadh and Abu Dhabi.

The two million euros of purchases or subscriptions, clearly coming in 2019 from Saudi Arabia and the United Arab Emirates, were aimed at supporting the "independent" group in exchange for preferential treatment for the policies pursued by Riyadh and Abu Dhabi. The objective of the Emirates and Saudi Arabia is clearly to influence French decision-makers, particularly in their relations with Qatar. It is therefore a form of foreign interference that the Indigo Group is participating in.

In conclusion, it is clear that, in a more or less consenting manner, France is fully integrated into the UAE's expansion strategy. Between established facts and active *lobbying*, historical relationships and new alliances, *soft power* and trade negotiations, a bipolar game of seduction pits Qatar against the UAE-Saudi Arabia duopoly, without the public always being aware of the underlying stakes. *Business*, politics, religion and battles of influence are part of a complex situation where ulterior motives and small arrangements are legion. Especially since the ambition of the UAE does not stop there...

17. From blue gold to clouds

Success or failure, compromise or success, nothing can stop it: water is a crucial problem for the United Arab Emirates, as it is for the other states of the Arabian Peninsula. Indeed, their main characteristic is to be a desert, apart from a few oases that have given rise to the establishment of cities such as Mecca, Medina or Riyadh ["The Gardens" in Arabic]. *Nihil novi sub sole*! The Saudi king Ibn Saud had asked American geologists attracted by the smell of oil to find him water in return for possible oil concessions, black gold financing blue gold.

For the Emirates, the problem of water is all the more crucial as the oil rent modifies behaviors and leads to an overconsumption of groundwater. It is estimated that Emiratis consume 390 liters per day per inhabitant for domestic use, compared to 250 liters per day for a French person, i.e. 26 times more water than they have available, i.e. approximately 34 m3 of water per year per inhabitant. The Emiratis have happily pumped into the water tables, including the so-called fossil water tables, which are not renewable in the short term since they were formed before the appearance of man.

The United Arab Emirates is therefore in a situation of advanced water stress. Water supply is increasingly struggling to keep up with demand, which is exploding with high population growth, fuelled by one of the world's highest rates of immigration. In fact, the federation's cities are becoming increasingly populated, and living standards are rising steadily. In addition, there is a growing agricultural practice of flood irrigation in the field, which allows a lot of water to evaporate. The processing industries are not to be outdone, requiring astronomical amounts of water to feed steel and aluminum plants.

The solutions envisaged to alleviate this problem are limited. The United Arab Emirates have had to invest in the costly process of desalination of sea water: 14% of the water made drinkable in the world is due to Abu Dhabi, just behind Ryad. Problem: "This dependence on desalination is neither bearable nor desirable," says Sultan Ahmed Al Jaber. Certainly, new technologies have made it possible to considerably reduce production costs. This is the case of "reverse osmosis" developed by Veolia, which requires less energy than distillation and accounts for one out of every five liters consumed in the country. However, although 2 kilowatts are enough to produce one cubic meter of fresh water, compared to 12 kilowatts in 1980, the final bill is still considered... expensive.

In other words, water desalination plants, which consume a lot of electricity, are not a sustainable solution to meet the growing needs of the population.

In addition to the cost, the environmental impact of desalination contributes to the doubts of the UAE authorities. Hence the development of "pilot projects" for desalination based on renewable energy. At the helm are four industrial groups, including the French companies Veolia and Suez Environnement, in the Abu Dhabi region, under the leadership of the Masdar ("the source" in Arabic) Sustainable City Institute, an eco-city project announced in 2006 and intended to accommodate up to 50,000 inhabitants and 1,500 companies once completed. Masdar is supposed to be the world's first "zero-carbon, zero-waste" city. The emirate has in mind a project for a sustainable desalination plant with a daily capacity of 150,000 m3 running on solar energy. Local recycling aims to reduce the consumption of desalinated seawater by 80%. The wastewater is to be used to irrigate crops for food and biofuel production; the city's landscaped areas are to be watered with the treated wastewater. Ten years after they took on this challenge, the failure is obvious. Indeed, the city is struggling to attract businesses. Only a few hundred students from the Masdar Institute live there, far from the tens of thousands of inhabitants expected.

The idea of building up strategic reserves of fresh water, just as Western countries build up strategic reserves of oil, was then imposed. The Emirates have thus embarked on Aquifer

17. From blue gold to clouds

Storage Recovery, which consists of injecting and storing desalinated water in empty underground aquifers. The German company GIZ IS is finalizing the construction of a project estimated at 500 million dollars on behalf of the Abu Dhabi Water and Electricity Authority (Adwea). The project aims to store some 26 million cubic meters underground in the Liwa oasis region. This will enable one million people to survive for 90 days in times of severe shortage, with a maximum daily consumption of 180 liters of drinking water per capita.

That's not stopping Abu Dhabi's *brainstormers*, from which some amazing projects are emerging. In May 2017, for example, an Abu Dhabi company floated the idea of towing icebergs from Antarctica to address the UAE's drinking water shortage. According to estimates by the National Advisor Bureau Limited, with its 75,000 billion liters of water, an iceberg could meet the drinking water needs of nearly one million people for five years. In a video presentation, the Emirati company aimed to illustrate its towing project, between Heard Island, located near Antarctica, and the city of Fujairah, in the Persian Gulf. In total, 10,000 km of crossing, through the Indian Ocean and the Arabian Sea. The feasibility of the operation is as questionable as the cost estimate: a simple traction boat can be worth up to $75,000 per day...

And this idea is not the craziest one to have been put forward! Consider instead that, on January 19, 2016, under the golds of the Emirates Palace in Abu Dhabi, Sultan Ahmed Al Jaber rewarded with great fanfare three foreign scientists for their work in the field of rainfall acceleration, supposedly to milk stratocumulus clouds to harvest their water. The budget allocated to the three so-called scientists - a German, a Japanese and a Chinese - for this Rain Enhancement Research Program? Five million dollars over three years.

This modern rain dance is therefore very serious and is based on an accounting estimate made by experts from the National Centre for Meteorology and Seismology (NCMS) of the United Arab Emirates. According to them, making rain fall would be cheaper than desalinating sea water. Even if the expected result is modest: "According to our calculations, we could increase the rainfall yield by at least 5%," says Alia Al Mazrouei, the program director at the CNMS. But rainfall in the United Arab Emirates is almost negligible. The country is among the driest in the world and can only count on an average of 78 millimeters of water per year (compared to 1,220 millimeters in Great Britain). Valuing a small increase in the country's rainfall resources at $5 million is perplexing, but it does betray the growing concern about water.

In fact, water is not only scarce because of the climate: its price is very low. Raising the cost of blue gold could help limit its expensive use. In Abu Dhabi, the idea is gradually gaining ground. A pricing system has been introduced to encourage users to monitor their consumption. However, the prices charged remain very low and out of all proportion to the urgency of the situation. Hence the interest of the UWSS for the Nile basin...

18. From Sudan to Ghana

In the eyes of MBZ, securing food for the United Arab Emirates requires a say in the situation in the Nile basin. In this perspective, Sudan can help consolidate many vital interests for the Gulf countries. This is why Khartoum appears as a central element on the East African chessboard. In the event of open conflict between Ethiopia and Egypt, Sudan could be a pivotal country. The possibility is taken seriously enough that the United Arab Emirates has purchased nearly 400,000 hectares of land in that country.

It must be said that the risk is not new. In 1978, after the Camp David peace accords, Anwar Sadat declared that water could push him to declare war on Mengitsu Haile Mariam, the Ethiopian president at the time, who was planning to build a dam on Lake Tana. But in April 2011, just after Mubarak's overthrow, Ethiopia launched a pharaonic and strategic project called the Renaissance Dam, located on the waters of the Blue Nile. This project, which has long been controversial, is set to be the largest dam in Africa, at a cost of nearly $6 billion. It is 170 meters high and about two kilometers wide and aims to produce 6,000 megawatts of electricity, three times as much as the Aswan Dam. The construction of this dam should allow Ethiopia to

- to irrigate his land,
- to prevent flooding,
- to satisfy its energy needs and to
- export electricity to neighboring countries such as Djibouti, Sudan and Kenya for more than 730 million euros per year.

Currently, water from the Ethiopian plateaus accounts for 86% of the water consumed in Egypt and 95% during flood periods. The Blue Nile alone provides 59% of the Nile's flow. The Renaissance Dam project would reduce the flow of the Nile in Egypt by 25%. Tensions between Egypt, Ethiopia and Sudan, 77% of whose inflow is linked to the Blue Nile, are unlikely to ease easily.

For the UAE, these structural issues are part of the broader problem of *land grabbing, as* we saw in Chapter 4. The objective of countries engaged in land grabbing is to secure access to food resources. Many states buy so-called *offshore* land. Alternatively, they obtain long leases in developing countries. Nearly half (47%) of the land grabbed is in Africa and a third (33%) in Asia.

In addition to the vampirization of land, there is also an indirect appropriation of water resources. Nearly 60% of the water is thus monopolized by companies from countries that practice *land grabbing* such as... the United Arab Emirates. Since 2009, the United Arab Emirates have acquired more than 1.3 million hectares, including

- 900,000 hectares[64] in Pakistan[65] ;

- nearly 400,000 in Sudan; and

- 3,000 in the Philippines.

In Mozambique, permit applications covering 607,236 hectares are under review. At the heart of these land purchases is National Holding, a United Arab Emirates company owned by the Abu Dhabi royal family. According to a Mozambican NGO, this project could result in the forced displacement of more than 500,000 families. The Emirates are also negotiating the acquisition of several hundred thousand hectares in Ukraine, the breadbasket of Eastern Europe.

However, as a priority, the Emirates are investing in the Sahelian areas where Westerners and jihadists compete for business. In August 2019, Mohamed bin Zayed invested $30

---

64. Florence Brondeau, "Les investisseurs étrangers à l'assaut des terres agricoles africaines", on *EchoGéo*, n°14, 2010.

65. Since 2009, some private companies, on behalf of the UAE government, have purchased 324,000 ha in Pakistan. They have purchased more than 15 ha in Balochistan near the Mirani Dam and hope to sign a memorandum of understanding with the local government. The UAE is also in negotiations with the Sindh provincial government to purchase land in Shikarpur, Larkana and Sukker. It has also expressed interest to the governments of Punjab and North West Frontier provinces. In Punjab, they want to invest in the area around Mianwali, Sardogha, Khushab, Jhang and Faisalabad. Source: http://www.cadtm.org/spip.php?page=imprimer&id_article=4436.

billion in the five G5 Sahel states of Mauritania, Niger, Burkina Faso, Chad and Mali, in exchange for two significant benefits:

- the construction of a military base in Niger and

- the selling off of gigantic wealth, especially in rare earths.

We know why, in the name of uranium, France is holding on to Mali. The UAE has even fewer scruples about extracting vast riches.

The loss of tax revenues from mining is considerable [for the countries of the region]. However, they benefit certain large groups listed on the stock exchange and based in Dubai, where the epicenter of this new reality is located: the Dubai Multi Commodities Centre (DMCC). This smuggling situation involves suspicious financial flows that impact the sovereignty of the African states concerned. The latter lose benefits for their economic development, their own security and the development of human potential.

In an April 24, 2019, dispatch, Reuters claims that billions of dollars worth of gold and other mineral resources are being smuggled out of Africa to the UAE and China. The British news agency goes further, claiming that this lucrative and illegal trade would fuel certain conflicts - including the one that has killed tens of thousands of Yemenis since 2015. It would violate human rights and endanger the environment of the countries in which these resources are extracted in total disregard of international trade rules and international law.[66]

Some countries are trying to protect themselves against the voracious appetite of China and now the UAE, but David cannot always win against Goliath! Especially since the UAE is also buying directly from local operators in Africa. Among the countries, Ghana is once again the focus of attention because, according to Human Rights Watch, 100% of the gold mined in Ghana, which is still resistant to foreign appetites, is mined by children on behalf of large multinational companies[67]. These include Indian and South African companies, as well as Emirates Gold and Kaloti Jewellery International. The financial voracity of the powerful, under the pretext of food, anti-terrorism or humanitarianism, is endless...

66. https://www.lepoint.fr/afrique/or-diamants-terres-rares-la-ruee-predatrice-vers-l-afrique-08-08-2019-2328983_3826.php
67. http://www.rfi.fr/afrique/20150612-eclat-or-ghana-terni-le-recours-travail-enfants-human-right-watch-mercure-minamata

19. From Israelization to the Emirate Leaks

In its struggle to survive and thrive, Abu Dhabi has a model: Israel. Surprising? Not really, because the Hebrew state resurrects MBZ's fantasy of a bastion state fighting for freedom against the rest of the region. Yes, the comparison may seem incongruous; absurd, no. Indeed, how can one preserve one's integrity in an aggressive and unfavourable geopolitical context, and pursue unparalleled economic and social development in the face of powerful enemies? Both share the vision of Iran as the ultimate enemy, what the Israelis call *amalek*[68].

A micro-state in the region, facing the sea and the land, Tel Aviv-Jaffa has risen politically as a criticizable, but undeniable, economic, scientific and military power. On March 28, 2019,

---

68. Amalek is the ultimate enemy of the Israelis, often equated with modern-day Iran. But the myth refers to mythology and the Holy Scriptures, when the twelve tribes of Israel, trying to flee from Egypt, were attacked gratuitously by Amalek and his tribe. Since then it has become the symbol of the gratuitous violence and the will to annihilate the Hebrew people.

in a speech to the American Jewish Congress, Anwar Gargash, UAE Minister of State for Foreign Affairs, made amends for the past, regretting the decades-long unfair boycott of Israel. For him, it was a grave mistake, and for good reason: today there is much more to share than to lose, especially by taking a leaf out of Israel's book for its own survival[69]. To the point that, in an interview we had with him in October 2019, Bassar Taham, a French-Syrian Islamologist and political scientist, did not hesitate to speak of the Israelization of Abu Dhabi...

> The Emirates is just one example of the Israelization of small Arab states, very small states, with dreams of grandeur. But the Emirates is a tiny country. In the light of what has happened in the Middle East, its leaders have understood that they must use money to become a strong state in every sense of the word: scientific, military (arms purchases, manufacturing, foreign policy) and economic (foreign investment). Israel indirectly becomes an ideal for these people. It is Israel's success that will make certain minorities in the country evolve towards the notion of a small, powerful and expansionist state.

In essence, Abu Dhabi understood that there would be no salvation without the emergence of an overpowered, armed and diverse emirate. Surprise: no one saw this coming, even in

---

69. https://www.timesofisrael.com/senior-uae-official-calls-for-strategic-shift-in-arab-israel-relations/

the most discerning Western circles working not far from Abu Dhabi. The city has become a fortress, winning new battles with Dubai for increasing control of ports around the world, training mercenary commandos in Africa to secure shipping lanes against pirates, especially in the Horn of the continent.

From Lebanon, that "Switzerland of the East" lost by its elites, financial power - power, in short - has shifted to the UAE. And the irresistible rise of the Emirati regional power in the Middle East took another step forward in August 2020, with the normalization of its relations with the Jewish state, under the name of the Abraham Accords. It is essentially a matter of forming a united front against Iran with Saudi Arabia; but it is also the realization of an old Emirati fantasy that also sees in Israel a model of exceptional development. In exchange for this friendship, a vague moratorium on the annexation of the Palestinian territories and the sweet mirage of a Palestinian state postponed to the Greek calendar.

However, there is nothing casual about this connection with Israel. If the United Arab Emirates has risen to the *top of* the regional rankings without the experts anticipating it, it is partly due to Abu Dhabi's exceptional ability to forge alliances that at first glance seem unnatural. Wouldn't it be shocking for an Arab country to ally itself with Israel? MBZ sees no problem with this, as the goal would be to join forces against the region's number one enemy: Iran. In return, Abu Dhabi benefits from the Israeli genius in terms of new information technologies, armaments, and security tools, especially

19. From Israelization to the Emirate Leaks

cybernetic, to ensure its survival and to rise higher and higher, but that is only fair!

UAE Israelization is based on the *start-up nation* model, which has made Emmanuel Macron himself fantasize, but which above all inspired MBZ to develop his country *through* the support provided

- to advanced industries,
- to the arms and security industries,
- to cyber protection,
- economic diversification and
- to investments *worldwide.*

The seduction enterprise is asymmetrical but reciprocal. As proof, in July 2019, the former Israeli foreign minister, Yisrael Katz had his picture taken on the esplanade of the Sheikh Zayed mosque, Katz, affirming Tel Aviv's interest in Emirati policy and not only in security matters[70]. On 1er November 2019, the Emirate Leaks evoke a desire for normalization firing all unofficial wood.

A delegation of Israeli high school students participated on Monday in the Dubai FIRST competition dedicated to robotics, in which representatives of the Hebrew state won four medals. The Israeli delegation won gold and silver medals, and qualified for the final stage to be held in the United States, where Italy, Uganda and Australia will also compete. Science and Technology Minister Ofir Akunis said that "they have

---

70. https://fr.timesofisrael.com/eau-israel-katz-evoque-liran-et-la-secur-ite-avec-un-responsable-a-abu-dhabi/

achieved unprecedented results" and that he "never doubted their ability to achieve excellent results.[71]

To understand what is at stake in this *seemingly* surprising alliance, we must go back to the *Panama Papers*. We learn that a certain Mati Kochavi, an Israeli businessman who made his fortune in real estate, became an outstanding arms dealer, playing the role of intermediary between the countries concerned. It was in the *post* 9/11 context that he created a cyber-surveillance empire with solutions combining cameras and state-of-the-art security barriers. Fearing an Iranian aggression, the United Arab Emirates called on Kochavi to equip and defend itself for, let's say, considerable sums.

Documents obtained by Haaretz in 2017 reveal a transaction worth three billion shekels (more than 760 million euros), part of which was allegedly paid in cash. This sum involves one of the group's subsidiaries and Emirati figures. A close examination of the leaked correspondence of the legal-financial firm Appleby reveals that the UAE army, very impressed by the performance of Israeli and British electronic intelligence aircraft, wanted to acquire this type of airborne capability in anticipation of a war against Iran.[72]

---

71. http://emiratesleaks.com/fr/une-normalisation-nette-des-Émirats united-arabes-with-israel/
72. https://mondafrique.com/laccord-darmement-entre-israel-et-mbz-le-prince-heritier-des-emirats/

19. From Israelization to the Emirate Leaks

Mohamed bin Zayed's interest in Israeli technology dates back to 2008 and the first major tensions with Iran. His goal was to begin cooperation between the two countries by upgrading two old civilian planes to turn them into spy planes over-equipped with surveillance equipment. But how does the link between the two countries work in practice for these two planes? Through a series of financial "arrangements" that pass through front companies. The Emirate Leaks that we have just quoted do not hide anything about it.

In the case of spy planes, the army chose an Abu Dhabi company, created in 2006 and owned by Abdullah Ahmed Al Balooshi, a person close to the intelligence services. Its name: Advanced Integrated Systems (AIS). Its specialty: the supply of security and surveillance systems. From the outset, the verification of documents reveals an invoice dated 2015, amounting to 629 million euros for the two equipped aircraft and their maintenance, or 80 million more than the initial arrangement between the UAE army and AIS dating from 2010. Sensors and their software dedicated to the interception of electronic signals (ELINT) for 65 million euros, long-range antennas and decryption software for the listening and interception of communications for 80 million euros, a self-protection system for the aircraft for 42 million euros, two long-range oblique cameras LOROP for more than 40 million euros, and a whopping 35 million euros for support and maintenance

AIS awarded the integration project to the Swiss company AGT International, owned by Mati Koshavi. Koshavi's company bought the equipment and then awarded the integration contract to the British firm Marshall for $100 million.

In addition to this transaction, Koshavi's company is also involved in one of the most sensitive areas in the UAE. It is AGT International that has supplied thousands of cameras, license plate readers and all the IT infrastructure for urban security management in Abu Dhabi and all the borders and entry points in the UAE. All this infrastructure is managed by an artificial intelligence system delivered by Wisdom, an Israeli company in charge of processing in real time millions of videos and images taken all over the country, without any guarantee that these data are not also under the control of other entities than the Emirati state.

The Israeli drifts in this matter are disturbing and give rise to fears about those of their new ally:
- offensive wars in Gaza resulting in thousands of deaths,
- targeted military interventions against its enemies,
- use of non-conventional weapons,
- state cyber attacks, etc.

The Emiratis seem to be following the same path while hoping for a status as a great regional political strategist, capable of discussing and negotiating with everyone. The reality is more complex, as relations with Iran would reveal to the skeptic.

19. From Israelization to the Emirate Leaks

In the summer of 2021, the scandal surrounding the Pegasus software, marketed by the Israeli company NSO, reinforced suspicions about the foundations of the strange link between the Hebrew state and the UAE. Damien Leloup and Martin Untersinger write it in black and white:

> Israel protects and pampers NSO, a tool of its *soft power*, the provision of which to governments has contributed to the restoration of diplomatic relations. NSO's activities shed some light on the Hebrew state's recent rapprochement with Saudi Arabia, Hungary or Morocco (...).[73]

Clearly, the rapprochement between certain States and Israel seems to be linked to the marketing of this spying tool, whose reefs are immense: 50,000 telephone numbers are likely to have been infected, including those of heads of state, opponents, activists, lawyers and journalists.

Abu Dhabi is one of the states particularly fond of the dreaded spyware. While MBZ and MBS are suspected of having been involved in the assassination of Jamal Kashoogi, Amnesty International's investigation was able to show that, thanks to the spyware, "the entourage of Jamal Khashoggi, the Saudi columnist for The *Washington Post who* was murdered on October 2, 2018 in Istanbul, Turkey, was under surveil-

---

731. https://www.lemonde.fr/projet-pegasus/article/2021/07/18/projet-pegasus-revelations-sur-un-systeme-mondial-d-espionnage-de-telephones_6088652_6088648.html

lance,"[74], specifically Hanan El-Atr, the Egyptian flight attendant with whom the journalist was in love, and Hatice Cengiz, the missing man's Turkish fiancée[75]. These elements confirm,

- on the one hand, the total disregard of certain Arab states for human rights;
- on the other hand, the importance of *soft power* in the region, intimately linked to the invention, the provision and the officially "diverted" use of technological weapons like Pegasus.

In the end, the problem is not so much the expertise sold by Israel, but rather the massive and misguided use made of it by certain Arab countries, which are therefore strongly encouraged to draw closer to the Hebrew state.

Today, Israel remains one of the beacons that seem to guide MBZ. Under its leadership, the Emiratis hope to follow Jerusalem's path to solid independence and a status as a major political strategist in the region, able to discuss and negotiate with everyone. However, the reality is more complex, as the chaotic relations between the UAE and Iran reveal.

---

74. https://www.lemonde.fr/projet-pegasus/article/2021/07/18/affaire-khashoggi-deux-femmes-proches-du-journaliste-assassine-ont-ete-surveillees-par-pegasus_6088655_6088648.html
75. https://www.franceculture.fr/geopolitique/affaire-khashoggi-larabie-saoudite-et-les-emirats-arabes-unis-ont-cible-son-entourage-apres-sa-mort

20. From Tehran to Paris

From 2016, facing Tehran, the strategic line is simple, in theory: it is to make Iran bend by multiplying sanctions and isolation measures. The support of the United States should make it possible to crush the nuclear impulses of the mullahs' regime. Except that, once again, after the failed blockade against Qatar, the UAE underestimated the capacity of its adversaries to resist. Fearing that tensions would inflame the region, MBZ finally tried to get closer to Iran.

In November 2019, Anwar Gargash, the Emirati Minister of State for Foreign Affairs, therefore advocated for a collective de-escalation supposedly to resolve the crisis. Beyond the rhetoric, it would seem that this sudden rapprochement is conditional on two changes in strategy for Abu Dhabi towards its neighbor: withdrawal from Yemen and securing the Gulf's sea. The logic is still the same - rather a stable dictatorship than a slide into disorder. And the economy has a lot to do with this change in posture. Indeed, Abu Dhabi has borne the brunt of the reinstated sanctions, as the Iranian community in Dubai plays a large economic role and is very powerful there. Before 2015, the city was even a second alternative port for Iranians in the face of U.S. sanctions.

There was a time in Dubai when, on both sides of the creek, the inlet that gave birth to the Gulf emirate, one could hear Persian as well as Arabic, English or Hindi. Dotted with banks, bazaars, mosques and Iranian restaurants, the districts of Deira and Bur Dubai, the historic center of the city-state, attracted a host of traders, entrepreneurs and tourists from the Islamic Republic in the 2000s. The tiny territory, which is part of the United Arab Emirates federation, served as a substitute port for the Persian giant, which was embargoed by the United States.[76]

After this complicit period, the multiplication of crises in the Gulf pushed the Iranians of Dubai to exile to Turkey and Oman. From 700,000, Iranians in the UAE dropped to 350,000. The same is now true for trade, which was valued at nearly $20 billion in 2018 and has halved. This means that nearly 10 billion in trade is taking place notwithstanding the sanctions regime, in full view of the US!

It was therefore necessary to show signs of appeasement between Abu Dhabi and Tehran as soon as possible. That is

---

76. https://www.lemonde.fr/international/article/2019/08/07/le-lent-et-silencieux-exode-des-iraniens-de-dubai_5497366_3210.html

why an Emirati delegation visited the Iranian capital during July 2019. Other parallel meetings took place in the same year.

The latest, on July 30, 2019, was a meeting on Iranian soil between the head of the Emirati coast guard and his counterpart in the Islamic Republic. During this meeting, the first of its kind in six years, the two men discussed cooperation and maritime security, a particularly sensitive subject at a time when sabotage and boarding of tankers are increasing in the Gulf.[77]

Since then, a border cooperation agreement has been signed between Iran and the UAE to maintain the security of movement in the Gulf. It is possible that in the coming months the relationship between the two countries will intensify as never before. Does this mean that the UAE could not care less about international disapproval in general and humanitarian law in particular? Obviously, the case is a tad more complicated. Human Rights Watch and Amnesty International regularly denounce the torture that the Emirati jails would have the secret but, right in its boots, the confederation blows cold and hot. In July 2012, the United Arab Emirates ratified the International Convention against Torture. Except that compliance with this convention remains questionable. In February 2014, Gabriela Knaul, the United Nations special

---

77. https://www.lemonde.fr/international/article/2019/08/07/sanctions-contre-l-iran-les-Émirats united-arabes-change-of-tactics-face-a-teheran_5497373_3210.html

rapporteur on the independence of judges and lawyers, did not mince her words at the end of a nine-day mission.

"I have received credible information and evidence that ... detainees were tortured and/or ill-treated," she said, denouncing "warrantless arrests of suspects taken blindfolded to unknown locations ... and held in solitary confinement, sometimes for months, and placed in the electric chair.

As evidence of the authorities' unease, she had not been able to work freely. "I was not allowed to visit the prisons and meet with some of the inmates I wanted to see," she said with regret. Unfortunate statements for a country concerned about its image? It would have taken more to disturb the serenity of the UAE authorities. Yet the 2018 Human Rights Watch global report did not see any improvement in the situation. "The government and the many public relations companies it pays to do so try to portray the UAE as a modern, reform-minded country," said Sarah Leah Whitson, director of the Middle East and North Africa division. "This optimistic vision will remain a fiction as long as the UAE refuses to release unjustly jailed activists, journalists and critics like Ahmed Mansoor."

Indeed, in March 2017, Abu Dhabi had detained Ahmed Mansoor, a well-known human rights activist who for years had vigorously defended dissidents who had been subjected to routine arbitrary arrests in that country. Mansoor faces freedom of expression charges, including using social media

United Arab Emirates conquering the world

to "spread false information that undermines national unity. It should be noted that government abuses are not only directed at nationals. British academic Matthew Hedges, for example, was sentenced to life imprisonment by the federal court in Abu Dhabi for spying for a foreign country and filed a complaint against the UAE with the United Nations for torture and ill-treatment. The doctoral student at Durham University in northeast England had been arrested at Dubai airport on May 5, 2018, before being pardoned and then released in November 2018 to avoid damaging the close relationship between London and Abu Dhabi. He was researching the UAE's foreign and domestic security policy after the 2011 Arab Spring.

His words refused to be Manichean: "I was never physically tortured but it was psychological and it was like torture," he told *The Times*. In a letter to the UN High Commissioner for Human Rights, Michelle Bachelet, Matthew Hedges' lawyer, Rodney Dixon QC, nonetheless said that the treatment Matthew Hedges underwent in the UAE violated his human rights and that he made his confession under pressure. In July 2019, another Briton, Ali Issa Ahmad claimed that he was arrested and tortured while on vacation in the UAE because he was wearing a Qatar shirt. He also filed a complaint with the United Nations.

In addition to the issues of torture, there is also the issue of the rights of migrant workers. As early as 2014, the Human Rights Watch organization denounced the numerous cases of

20. From Tehran to Paris

servitude in which foreign domestic workers were placed[78]. In 2018, the same NGO persisted and signed by expanding its denunciations. Thus, it attested that construction workers who had emigrated to the UAE were victims of serious exploitation.

To be sure, the United Arab Emirates passed a domestic workers law in September 2017 that was supposed to go into effect in December 2017. For the first time, a law recognizes rights for migrant workers, but some provisions are weaker than those provided for other assets. Although employers are required to pay the cost of hiring migrant domestic workers, some employers believe it is appropriate to puncture what is owed to workers in the event that they ask to leave before their contract ends, protesting abusive conditions. This is the subtlety of the law: it prohibits recruitment agencies from charging fees to migrant workers, but it does not prohibit employers from doing so. Conversely, when workers choose to terminate their employment without breach of contract, the law requires them to compensate their employer with one month's salary.

The issue of human rights poisons even the ties with France, whose commitment to these issues is nevertheless eminently flexible. In November 2018, two complaints were filed in France for "complicity in torture" and "war crimes," even as MBZ was meeting with Emmanuel Macron. Ironically,

---

78. https://www.hrw.org/fr/news/2014/10/22/emirats-arabes-unis-pris-es-au-piege-exploitees-et-maltraitees

the first came from Qatari nationals who accused MBZ of "complicity in acts of torture" and "enforced disappearance" at the crimes against humanity and war crimes unit of the Paris prosecutor's office. The plaintiffs claim to have been "detained and tortured by agents of the State Security of the United Arab Emirates between February 2013 and May 2015," according to their lawyer Pierre-Olivier Sur.

By virtue of its "universal jurisdiction" for the most serious crimes, French justice has the ability to "prosecute and convict the perpetrators and accomplices of these crimes when they are on French territory," said Sur. The second complaint was filed by six Yemenis in association with the International Alliance for the Defense of Rights and Freedoms (AIDL). Since March 2015, Human Rights Watch has documented 87 attacks "illegal" under international law perpetrated by the anti-Houthi coalition, some of which can be likened to war crimes, causing nearly 1,000 civilian casualties.

As noted above, despite its clumsy denials, the United Arab Emirates is implicated in human rights abuses in Yemen, through its direct interventions, its support for so-called loyalist forces, and its operation of at least two *in situ* detention facilities. Their officials appear to have demanded the continued detention of individuals despite orders for their release, as well as the enforced disappearance of individuals and the transfer abroad of high-ranking detainees, according to research by Human Rights Watch. Former detainees and their family members reported violations or torture in facilities run by the United Arab Emirates and the proxy forces it supports[79]. Yemeni activists who have criticized these abuses have been threatened, harassed, detained, and disappeared.

HRW is not alone in exposing these scandals and the unhealthy complicity of the United States. In a report released on July 12, 2018, Amnesty International denounces the widespread use of torture and other ill-treatment in secret prisons[80]. Part of the Total gas liquefaction plant in Balhaf, which has been idle since the war began in 2015, was reportedly commandeered by the UAE at the official request of the Yemeni government and has been set up by them since mid-2017 as a detention facility. For the past two years, testimonies collected by Amnesty International, the UN panel of experts on Yemen, as well as Yemeni NGOs and activists have reported the existence of this detention facility. From then on, the UAE has only one solution: to try to impose itself in international organizations in order to maximize its zone of influence and limit the revelations on its abuses...

---

79. https://www.hrw.org/news/2017/06/22/yemen-uae-backs-abusive-local-forces, and https://www.ohchr.org/Documents/Countries/YE/A_HRC_39_43_EN.docx and https://www.hrw.org/fr/news/2018/01/18/emirats-arabes-unis-violations-graves-des-droits-humains-linterieur-et-lexterieur-du
80. https://www.amnesty.org/fr/latest/news/2018/07/disappearances-and-torture-in-southern-yemen-detention-facilities-must-be-investigated-as-war-crimes/

21. From failures to prospects

No matter how well you plan, sometimes plans fail. However, for MBZ, everything was set up. Considerable resources, in terms of *lobbying*, had been put on the table to enable the UAE to take over the presidency of the International Civil Aviation Organization at the end of November 2019. For months, Aysha Al Hameli, the UAE's first female pilot, led the campaign for her candidacy. Unfortunately, the *timing* was unfavorable to her. The blockade of Qatar, which began in June 2017, was fatal for her.

By banning Qatar Airways aircraft from Saudi, UAE, Bahraini and Egyptian airspace, the UAE thought it would bend its neighbor. However, despite heavy financial losses on some 20 routes, the Qatari national airline has taken advantage of this regional handicap to boost the opening of its routes, particularly those to Africa. Thus, 24 new routes have been inaugurated as of 2018. Since 2017, Akbar Al-Baker, the chairman of Qatar Airways, had asked the International

Civil Aviation Organization (ICAO) to denounce the blockade against his country which violated the international convention on air transport. In vain.

From May 21 to June 21, 2019 takes place the 40e assembly of the ICAO, created in 1944 and whose headquarters is in Montreal. In addition to the General Secretariat, the organization is made up of

- of the board,
- of the air navigation commission and
- of the assembly.

The Council is composed of 36 permanent members elected every three years and have been meeting since late September 2019 to consider candidates for the next presidency. The election is scheduled for November 25, 2019. The multiplication of crises in which the Emirates and their Saudi ally are involved, such as the non-resolution of the issue of the blockade against Qatar - recognized as illegal by the United Nations - leave a small chance for Ms. Al Hameli to accede to the leadership of an organization for which her country of origin has little regard. Indeed, legally speaking, the UAE as of 2017 has clearly violated the ICAO constitution under the 1944 Chicago Convention. They violated the air transit agreement and transferred weapons in civilian aircraft to war zones in which they are involved. Yemen, for example.

Ms. Al Hameli has been the UAE's representative on the Council for many years, and Qatar has never seen any desire on her part to resolve their dispute for over two years. Once elected, she would still be clearly under the instructions of her government. The Organization would have lost all credibility if the Council Chair had belonged to one of the parties involved in an international air transport dispute. ICAO has therefore elected Salvatore Sciacchitano to manage the future of an industry that is set to become increasingly important in terms of passenger flows, the environment and global security.

Nevertheless, the Emirates are not the kind of people who get hot under the collar at the slightest drop of cold water. Obstinate, they try to place their pawns and influential people from their country within international institutions, ignoring international law. As a result, some disreputable people, accused of torture, find themselves in a position to run for the highest responsibilities, such as those of the director of Interpol, the international criminal police organization based in Lyon. This is the case of General Ahmed Nasser el Raissi, Inspector General of the UAE police. The man was previously accused by two British citizens of deliberately concealing acts of torture committed against them, but he was almost the only candidate. The reason is simple.

In recent years, ties between the UAE and Interpol have grown stronger. In 2016, the UAE donated 50 million euros to the organization. Interpol had a budget of 140 million euros in 2019, so the UAE has become the second largest contributor to Interpol, behind the United States[81] .

---

81. https://www.franceinter.fr/emissions/l-interview/l-interview-14-no-vembre-2020

21. From failures to prospects

Therefore, how can they be denied such honors and reward? In 2018, during the 87e session of the General Assembly of Interpol, Nasser Al Raissi was elected as an executive member of the organization. He will not land the president's scepter. The case of Matthew Hedges may have ended up tipping the scales against him. Arrested in Dubai and accused of espionage, the researcher was imprisoned for many months in the Emirates, tortured and sentenced to life imprisonment, then pardoned thanks to the anger of London. Nasser el Raissi, director of the police, was necessarily aware of this: one does not incarcerate European nationals in silence, from an international airport, without the hierarchy being informed. The UAE has again failed in its policy of entryism... but how long will common sense rules keep Abu Dhabi's emissaries in a reasonable place?

Nothing is set in stone, and the failures of the past do not foreshadow the future. Certainly, the war in Yemen waged by "the world's seventh army" since 2014 has been a total failure, as has the blockade against Qatar undertaken in June 2017 until January 2021. To compensate for the political radicalization of the country, the great plan for economic diversification and development planned for 2030 anticipated a wind of liberalization. The plan seems to have lost momentum as soon as it was implemented. The assassination of Jamal Kashoggi in Istanbul in October 2018 buried it, and it is not clear that allowing Saudi women to drive their own cars will be enough to resurrect it.

On September 14, 2019, the attack on Saudi Arabia's jewel Aramco refinery showed the limit of the omnipotence of sister states. Claimed by Yemen's Houthis, attributed to Iran, the work of a few missiles and drones proved

- the ineffectiveness of Saudi anti-aircraft batteries,
- the limits of the world's oil giant and, beyond the bluster,
- the fragility of the feet of clay that Riyadh and Abu Dhabi are trying to conceal.

For their part, the United Arab Emirates, caught up in their support for democratic counter-revolutions, are very busy imposing or maintaining the return to a security and authoritarian order from Sudan to Algeria, via Mauritania, Libya, Syria and Egypt. The withdrawal from Yemen has weakened Saudi Arabia, although the abuses have not really stopped[82]. However, MBZ sees further ahead. Seemingly unaffected by his many failures, the Crown Prince continues to dream of being master of the Muslim world. The collapse of the Gulf Cooperation Council opens a boulevard for him. The Sultanate of Oman and Kuwait, traditional *peacemakers,* have not succeeded in reviving this community body, and the figure of the Iranian enemy is struggling to convince. Wouldn't it be better to support the country from a transhistorical perspective as defined by lawyer and geopolitical expert Ardavan Amir Aslani[83]? Like it or not, Iran cannot be reduced

---

82. https://lemonde-arabe.fr/26/04/2020/arabie-saoudite-et-emirats-arabes-unis-faire-plier-le-yemen-par-tous-les-moyens-et-dans-lombre-de-lactualite/
83. *From Persia to Iran. 2500 years of history*, L'Archipel, 2018.

to its current government. The country belongs to its youth, who aspire to democracy and peace.

In Global Fire Power's 2019 report, Iran is ranked 14e world military power, ahead of Israel. For three millennia, the borders of this state have hardly changed. It has been one of the most stable regimes in the region for forty years. Its force is estimated at 400,000 men, 250,000 conscripts, nearly 400,000 Revolutionary Guards. 2,000 armoured vehicles as well as Russian and Chinese missiles provide it with a significant defensive capability. Certainly, from a Western perspective, one can be offended by its democratic shortcomings; pragmatically, however, the region needs stability. A healthy transition can only ever be made smoothly. Seeking to provoke chaos in Iran would lead to a catastrophe. Yet, Gerd Nönnemann, a professor of political science at Georgetown University in Doha, told me in October 2019, the UAE's position makes the future very worrying.

This will not end well, as tensions are rising and the demonstrations have all the same reasons. The actions of MBZ and its allies are likely to favour the Islamist currents once again. Even Marshal Haftar has failed in Libya. A further collapse is only a matter of time, and it would be all the more distressing because it would be in line with the authoritarian policies of Mohamed bin Zayed. The arrival of China and Russia in this quagmire will not bring anything positive. These states will support regimes that are similar to them, and therefore authoritarian regimes. MBZ is formidable. It will not hesitate to sow chaos in the region to the end for its own interests. Alas! We were also all talking to Saddam Hussein and Bashar Al Assad until…

It is not certain that America, partly disengaged from the region and focused on what Barack Obama called the Asian "pivot", can or wishes to change the situation by containing the merchant empire *of the* United States, connected to the strategic geopolitical triad of
- the Arabian Sea,
- the Persian Gulf and
- the Indian Ocean.

If one ventures to propose prospective avenues, one could imagine that the Emirates will see their role as regional security agent reinforced by delegation from Washington. The imperial dream of Mohamed bin Zayed, who knows exactly how to integrate and weigh in the future great global balances, is perhaps about to see the light of day in the era of the return of the great regional powers and bilateralism. It would become a bridge and a hinge between the West and China, on the famous new silk roads. The Emirates' conquest of the region's major ports was one of the planned steps in this global project. It has been successfully completed. Unfortunately, it is not certain that, in the name of regional stability and world security, we have reason to rejoice.

Appendix:
MBZ's men of influence

Anwar Gargash

Anwar Gargash, who comes from a prominent Dubai business family, is foreign minister. He is at the helm of much of the aggressive communication in favor of his country in the world.

He studied at George Washington University and taught at the University of the UAE. Since 2008, he has been the country's Foreign Minister and never fails to remind the three criteria of Emirati policy:

- valuing stability (even if it is authoritarian),
- justification of any exaction by the fight against terrorism, and
- opposition to Iran.

Thus he expressed himself, on May 18, 2019, in the *Journal du Dimanche*, presenting his "solution for Libya".

If there is one thing we have learned about the modern Middle East, it is that the region rarely succeeds in its political transitions and revolutions. They are most often violent, with chaotic melees overtaking peaceful power change. Fragile states collapse and become failed states, where the most ruthless actors like al-Qaeda and Daech benefit, as does Iran, which plays a disruptive role in the region. In this bleak landscape, we in the United Arab Emirates have charted a different course. Our system of government has provided stability and prosperity for our citizens.[84]

Saif ben Zayed Al Nahyan

Since October 2004, Saif bin Zayed has been Minister of Interior of the United Arab Emirates, responsible for the protection of the interior and internal security of the United Arab Emirates. He is also Deputy Prime Minister since May 10, 2009.

Abdullah ben Zayed Ben Sultan Al Nahyan

Minister of Foreign Affairs and International Cooperation since February 9, 2006, received by foreign chancelleries, he carries the UAE's word internationally. In August 2017, he had urged Iran and Turkey to stop what the UAE had called "colonial" actions in Syria. On February 14, 2019, he had

---

84. https://www.lejdd.fr/International/tribune-notre-solution-pour-la-lib-ye-par-le-chef-de-la-diplomatie-des-Émirats Arabes Unis-3899310

said that Israel was within its rights to attack Iranian targets in Syria. Thus, he is also part of the rapprochement between the UAE and Israel. He is a member of the National Security Council, vice chairman of the Standing Committee on Borders, chairman of the National Media Council, chairman of the board of directors of the Emirates Youth Development Foundation, vice chairman of the board of directors of the Abu Dhabi Development Fund, and a member of the board of the National Defense College.

Tahnoun ben Zayed Al Nahyan

A national security advisor, he is often portrayed as the UAE's spymaster. According to the UAE newspaper *Al Khaleej Online*, in mid-January 2019, senior UAE and Israeli officials took a private plane from Abu Dhabi to Tel Aviv to fly over Saudi airspace to Ben Gurion Airport. The plane was returning Israeli officials to Tel Aviv after a secret visit to Abu Dhabi in preparation for a supposed "surprise visit" by Abdullah bin Zayed Al Nahyan. This trip was supposed to precede the visit of the Israeli Prime Minister to the United Arab Emirates. The two trips did not take place, but this information indicates the closeness of contacts between the two countries.

Yousef Al Otaiba

He is the "damned soul" of MBZ. Currently the UAE's ambassador to the United States and minister of state, Al Otaiba has served as non-resident ambassador to Mexico.

Appendix: MBZ's men of influence

His father was the first oil minister of the United Arab Emirates and was elected president of OPEC six times. In this regard, he is considered one of the country's non-royal founding members, as well as a close confidant of the late founder Zayed Ben Sultan Al Nahyan (1918-2004).

Yousef Al Otaiba was raised in Cairo and was later selected for the Industrial College of the Armed Forces (ICAF) International Fellowship at the *National Defense University* in Washington, DC. Former CENTCOM commander General Anthony Zinni was one of his mentors. At age 26, Al Otaiba became the senior advisor to Mohammed bin Zayed, director of international affairs at the crown prince's court and the country's chief liaison on security, counterterrorism, and defense matters. In 2006 and 2007, Kristofer Harrison, U.S. State Department advisor on defense and government in the United States, described Al Otaiba's role as "critical in helping other countries in the region support President George W. Bush's troops," a role that was confirmed by Richard Burr, chairman of the Senate Intelligence Committee.

On June 22, 2008, Al Otaiba was appointed UAE ambassador to the United States. Upon his arrival in the capital, as ambassador, he worked closely with Howard Berman, then chairman of the House Foreign Affairs Committee, on an agreement that would allow the UAE to obtain nuclear materials from the United States for a civilian program. In July 2010, comments made by Al Otaiba were interpreted as

United Arab Emirates conquering the world

supporting a U.S. military strike against nuclear reactors in Iran[85].

Starting in 2015, Al Otaiba became one of the leading voices in Washington promoting the war in Yemen. He comes across as an effective ambassador as his country asserts itself more aggressively in foreign policy. In November 2017, he was promoted to minister of state, while remaining ambassador to the United States.

Al Otaiba is at the center of a massive email hacking case against it. In early June 2017, a group of *hackers* began distributing stolen emails to Al Otaiba's inbox. According to *The Intercept*, the leaked emails - possibly courtesy of hackers working for Qatar, according to The *New York Times* - revealed how the UAE supported the transfer of the U.S. Al Udeid airbase from Qatar, and how Al Otaiba had consolidated UAE influence in Washington. In 2015, the UAE reportedly paid $13.5 million to U.S. *lobbying* firms, including

- 6.5 million to the Camstoll Group, which was operated by former U.S. Treasury officials responsible for Gulf State and Israeli relations and counterterrorism financing, and
- 4.5 million to Harbour Group.

The documents leaked to the *Wall Street Journal* also allegedly implicate Al Otaiba in the multi-billion dollar corruption scandal surrounding Malaysia's state-run 1Malaysia Development Berhad, which allegedly netted Al Otaiba-

---

85. https://www.theguardian.com/world/2010/jul/07/uae-envoy-iran-nuclear-sites

connected companies $66 million, or 57.7 million euros, in *offshore* accounts.

The icing on this strange cake: in November 2017, leaked emails showed that Al Otaiba had allegedly hired *Havilland* Bank to develop a plan on how to unleash a financial war against Qatar, which has been banned from the GCC since June 5, 2017.

Mohammed ben Rachid Al Maktoum

At 70, the man is the Emir of Dubai, vice president, prime minister and minister of defence. A member of the Al Maktoum family, from the Bani Yas tribe, another branch of which rules Abu Dhabi, he trained in the military before being appointed head of the Dubai police and defense force.

Mansour ben Zayed Al Nahyan

He is the first brother of the current Crown Prince, Mohammed bin Zayed, and is Deputy Prime Minister and Minister of Presidential Affairs. He is also the half-brother of the current president of the federation. In 1997, he was appointed chairman of his father's presidential office. Upon his father's death, he was appointed by his elder half-brother, Khalifa bin Zayed Al Nahyan, as the first Minister of Presidential Affairs, merging the Presidential Office and the Presidential Court. He also held various positions in Abu Dhabi to support his brother, Crown Prince Mohammed bin Zayed Al Nahyan. He was appointed chairman of the

Ministerial Services Council, which is considered a ministerial entity attached to the cabinet.

In 2004, he became Minister of Presidential Affairs. In 2005, he became Vice Chairman of the Abu Dhabi Education Council (ADEC), Chairman of the Emirates Foundation, the Abu Dhabi Food Control Authority and the Abu Dhabi Development Fund. In 2006, he was appointed Chairman of the Abu Dhabi Judicial Department. In 2007, he was appointed Chairman of the Khalifa bin Zayed Charity Foundation. He is also the chairman of the Emirates Horse Racing Authority (EHRA), the Emirates horse racing authority, the horse being his hobby. Indeed, Mansour ben Zayed is an accomplished horseman and has won numerous endurance tournaments held in the Middle East. He is an avid supporter of Arabian horse racing, and the patron of the annual Zayed International Half Marathon competition in Abu Dhabi. On May 11, 2009, he was appointed Deputy Prime Minister while retaining his position as Minister of Presidential Affairs in the Royal Cabinet.

Sultan Ahmed Al Jaber

He is a Minister of State, Managing Director and CEO of the Abu Dhabi National Oil Company (ADNOC Group), Chairman of *Masdar City*, Chairman of the National Media Council. He is a strong advocate of alternative energy and sustainable development. However, on February 15, 2016, he was appointed CEO of ADNOC. He played a key role in the creation and launch of Masdar in 2006 and has served in various CEO roles. He has served as Masdar's chairman since March 2014 and was previously its managing director. Prior to Masdar, Sultan Ahmed Al Jaber worked on projects in the energy, utilities and other sectors at Mubadala Development Company. Masdar is a wholly owned subsidiary of Mubadala.

In 2009, Al Jaber was appointed by UN Secretary General Ban Ki-Moon to his Advisory Group on Energy and Climate Change (AGECC), which released its final report in 2010. Al Jaber's work on renewable energy and clean technologies led to his appointment in 2010 as the UAE's special envoy for energy and climate change. As Special Envoy, Al Jaber was responsible for helping to formulate and advocate the UAE's diplomatic and public policy positions on energy and climate change.

In 2011, Al Jaber was selected to serve on the United Nations Secretary-General's High Level Panel on Renewable Energy for All. This is an effort initiated by former UN Secretary General Ban Ki-moon to ensure universal access to modern utilities, double energy efficiency and global renewable energy market share by 2030.

In 2012, Al Jaber was elected "Champion of the Earth" by the United Nations. In 2013, he was named a Commander of the British Empire and Minister of State, establishing himself as the federation's Mr. Energy Transition.

Mohammed Dahlan

Mohammed Dahlan is the former head of preventive security in Gaza and former rival of Mahmoud Abbas for the presidency of the Palestinian Authority. A strongman in the Emirates for years with a wealth of security experience, he found refuge in Abu Dhabi in 2011 when the Palestinian Authority expelled him from Palestine, accusing him of plotting against President Abbas.

For forty years, Dahlan's story has been linked to that of Palestine. He is a man who has always been willing to do anything to lead his country, worthy of the decades during which the PLO did not balk at any bribe to do the same. Accused of corruption by Ramallah since 2016, wanted by Interpol, he continues to sink a golden exile in the United Arab Emirates. In 2016, some rumors even accused Abu Dhabi of wanting to provoke a coup in Palestine to place Mohammed Dahlan.

Today, Dahlan's priority seems to be to fight the Hamas Islamists who ousted him in 2007 and to retake Gaza (which Qatar is supporting financially against the chaos by funding part of the salaries of the officials providing security). In 2017, his shadow loomed over Gaza.

> The 56-year-old former head of Palestinian counter-terrorism, banished from the territory since Hamas expelled Fatah forces in 2007, is one of the main players in a major geopolitical game. A Palestinian-Egyptian-Emirati chess game aims to take back the leadership of the Palestinian coastal strip from the Islamists, who

have been crushed by a ten-year blockade and three wars against Israel. It was Dahlan himself who launched these major maneuvers at the beginning of the summer. With the financial support of the United Arab Emirates, the former strongman of Gaza began to pour cash into the Palestinian enclave. With Cairo's support, the outlaw even promised to ease the embargo by reopening the Rafah terminal at the gates of the Egyptian Sinai. In exchange, the ambitious colonel was to return to his native land and take control of civil affairs, with the Islamists content to manage security.[86]

In addition, Dahlan has multiplied structures posing as research centers in Europe although they are only a tool of influence and *lobbying for* the benefit of the United Arab Emirates. A singular detail: since 2015, Dahlan has had a Serbian passport.

---

86. https://www.lemonde.fr/international/article/2017/10/06/de-gaza-a-abou-dhabi-l-ascension-de-l-intrigant-mohammed-dahlan_5197098_3210.html

Table of contents

Best sellers Max Milo Editions

Hitler's banker, Jean-François Bouchard

Confessions of a forger, Éric Piedoie Le Tiec

The Koran and the flesh, Ludovic-Mohamed Zahed

Governing by fake news, Jacques Baud

Governing by chaos, Collectif

A political history of food, Paul Ariès

Mad in U.S.A.: The ravages of the "American model",
Michel Desmurget

Mondial soccer club geopolitics, Kévin Veyssière

Putin: Game master?, Jacques Braud

Treatise on the three impostors: Moses, Jesus, Muhammad,
The Spirit of Spinoza

TV Lobotomy, Michel Desmurget